Modelling Clay Animals

with 3 basic shapes

04414198

SCRIBBLERS

Contents

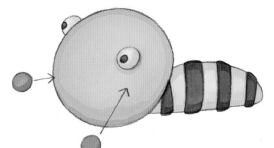

MATERIALS

You don't need special tools for working with modelling clay. You only need things like straws, a roller, toothpicks, paintbrushes, lids, markers, marbles, card, thick nylon wires, twigs...

Techniques

MAKING NEW COLOURS

You can use the colours as they are and create your own colours, too. Mix two or more colours together by kneading them until they blend into one colour. It's fun to invent your own new colours!

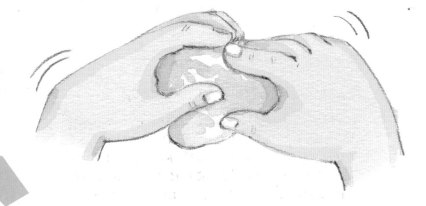

4

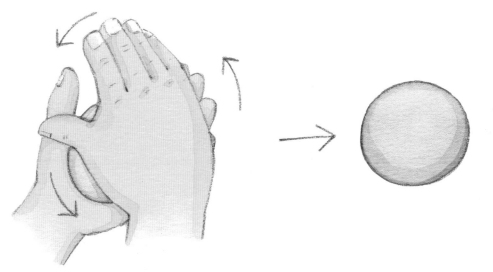

HOW TO MAKE A BALL SHAPE

Take some modelling clay between the palms of your hands and roll it around, pressing it into a round ball shape. If you need to, smooth it all over with your fingertips.

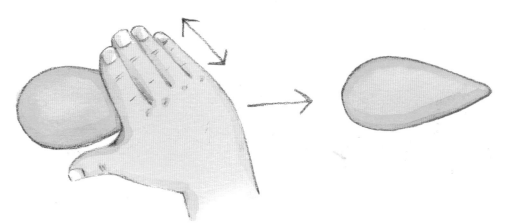

HOW TO MAKE A TEARDROP SHAPE

First make a ball, as above. Then put it on the table top and press down on one side only. Keep rolling backward and forward. You can make it smoother with your fingertips. If you cut off the round end to make a flat base, you'll have a cone. A cone can be made into a triangle by flattening the sides.

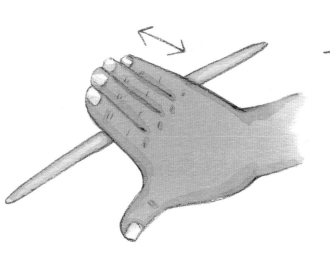

HOW TO MAKE A WORM SHAPE

Once again, you will start with a ball. Then roll it on the table top. Keep your fingers flat as you roll the modelling clay back and forward. Keep rolling it out until you have a worm shape of the thickness you need.

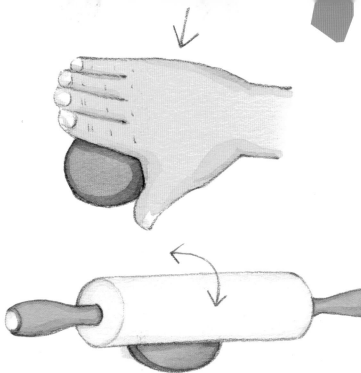

FLAT SHAPES

Use the palm of your hand to squash a modelling clay shape onto the table top. If the shape is small, you can flatten it between your fingers. If you want to make it really thin and even, you could use a roller. Remember to put paper down first so the modelling clay doesn't stick to the table.

SPOTS & STRIPES

If you flatten little balls of one colour onto a different coloured shape, you'll get spots. And if you flatten little worms onto a different colour, they turn into stripes.

JOINING TWO COLOURS

After joining two different coloured pieces, smooth the joint over with your fingers or roll it (if you can) with the flat of your hand.

CUTTING

To cut pieces of modelling clay, you can use a piece of strong card.

6

STRENGTHENING

When joining two pieces of modelling clay together, strengthen the joint from behind. Use your finger to smooth the clay, easing it down to overlap the joint. This will bond the pieces together well.

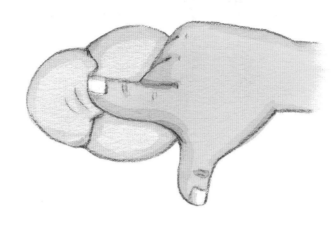

MARKS, DENTS AND LINES

Card is very useful for indenting straight or curved marks in modelling clay. You can also use toothpicks to add on shapes and lines.

HOLES

Depending on the size of the hole you need to make, you can use different things. A toothpick is good for tiny holes, the point of a pencil makes different sized holes (depending on how far you insert it), the end of a paintbrush makes medium-sized holes and a marker or marble makes large round holes.

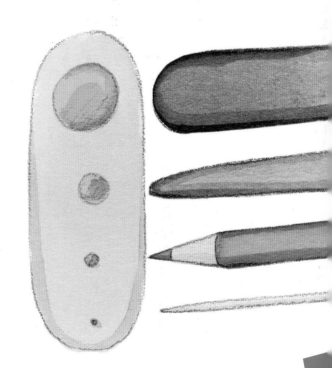

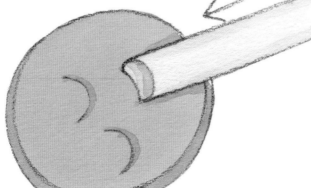

FACES AND TEXTURES

Plastic straws work really well for making little mouths and closed eyes. They're also great for making textures like fish scales and feathers. Stick them into the modelling clay straight or at an angle. Experiment and find what works best!

I'm a rhino

1. Roll some modelling clay into a ball for rhino's body. Then make a smaller ball in a lighter colour. Now cut it in half and stick it onto his body.

2. Make four little balls for his legs. Press them on well so that his body is stable.

3. Use the point of a pencil to make two holes in his snout and then add two tiny black balls for his eyes.

4. Use a piece of card to indent the shape of his mouth. Make the ears out of two teardrop-shapes and press on top of his head.

5. Roll a little bit of modelling clay between your hands to make a thin tail. And, last and most important for a rhinoceros – his horn! Make it out of a small white teardrop shape.

I love my horn

1. Make a yellow ball for Derek's head and a larger teardrop shape for his body. Stick the two pieces together.

2. Roll out a small orange log shape. Squash it a bit and cut off one end. Stick it to Derek's head to make his beak.

My name is Derek the **Duck**

3. Roll two little white balls and flatten them. Now stick them to each side of the head, for eyes.

4

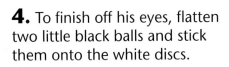

5. Now make two small teardrop shapes and flatten them slightly to make Derek's wings. Stick one onto each side of his body.

5

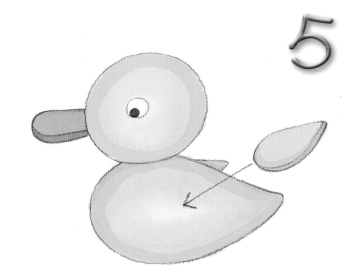

4. To finish off his eyes, flatten two little black balls and stick them onto the white discs.

Quack.... Does anyone want to play with me?

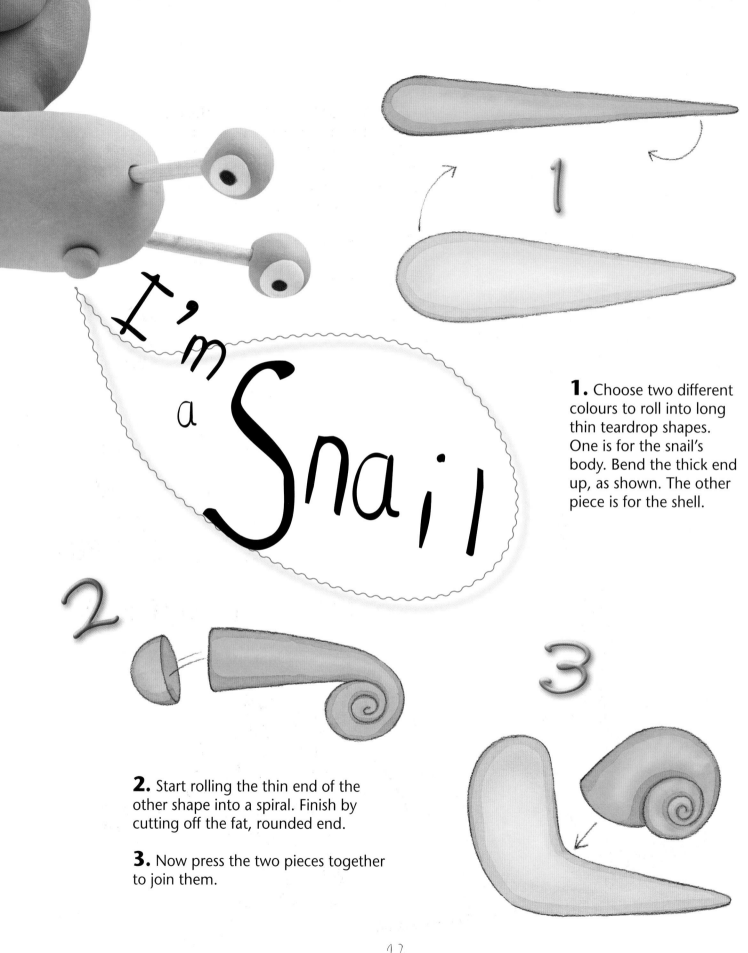

I'm a Snail

1. Choose two different colours to roll into long thin teardrop shapes. One is for the snail's body. Bend the thick end up, as shown. The other piece is for the shell.

2. Start rolling the thin end of the other shape into a spiral. Finish by cutting off the fat, rounded end.

3. Now press the two pieces together to join them.

4. You'll need three different coloured balls to make each eye: one the same colour as the body, one white and another tiny black one. Make up both eyes and use two pieces of toothpicks for stalks. Press them into the head.

5. Make a tiny nose with a little ball the same colour as the body. Stick it on for the final touch.

4

5

Mmm . . . I want a

big juicy leaf to eat

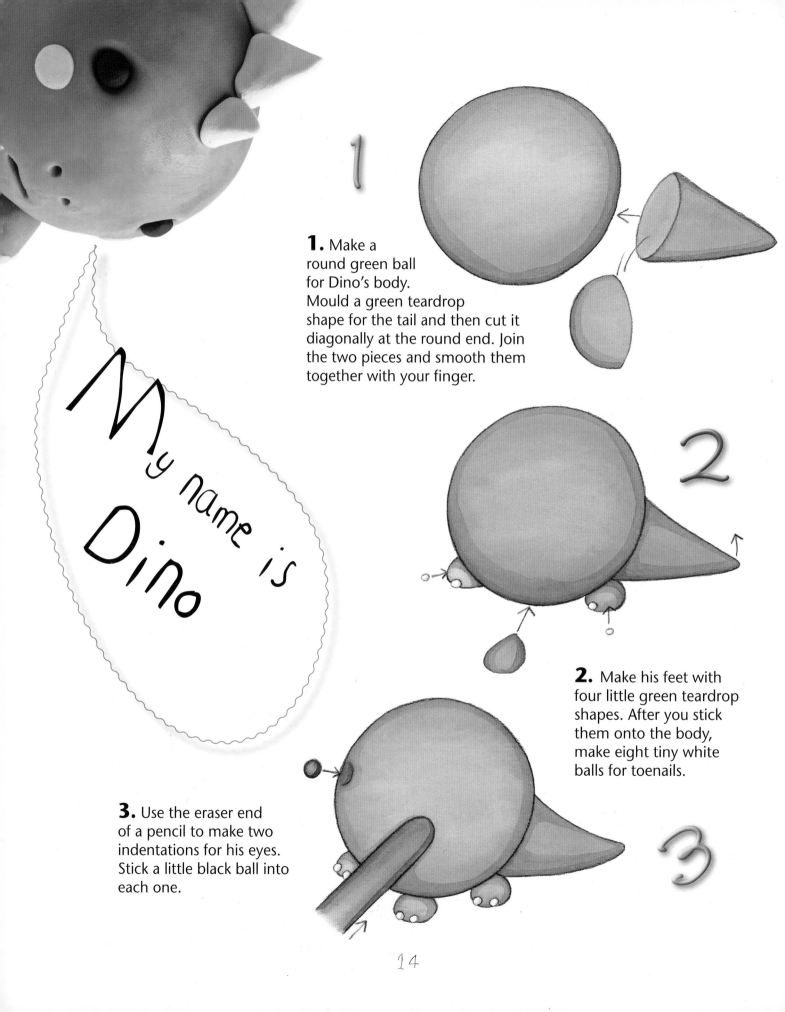

My name is Dino

1. Make a round green ball for Dino's body. Mould a green teardrop shape for the tail and then cut it diagonally at the round end. Join the two pieces and smooth them together with your finger.

2. Make his feet with four little green teardrop shapes. After you stick them onto the body, make eight tiny white balls for toenails.

3. Use the eraser end of a pencil to make two indentations for his eyes. Stick a little black ball into each one.

14

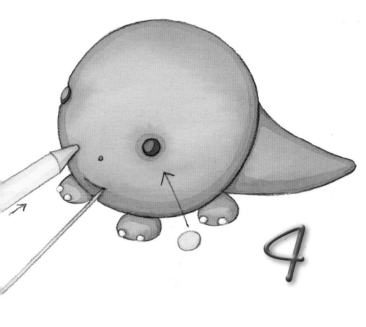

4. Draw in the mouth shape with a toothpick and make two holes for nostrils using the point of a pencil. You can give him blushed cheeks by sticking on two flat pink discs.

5. Now you just need to sculpt little triangle shapes to make the spikes on his back. They look nice in a different colour. Stick the longest edge of each triangle onto his back, from his head to the end of his tail.

I like to swish my tail!

I'm a bear

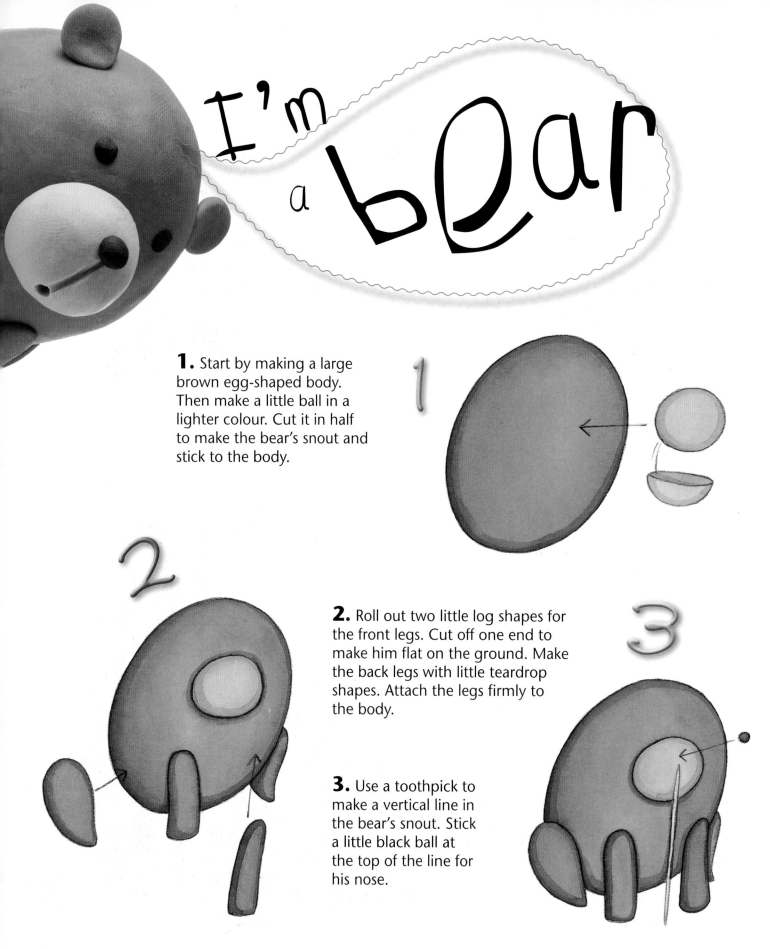

1. Start by making a large brown egg-shaped body. Then make a little ball in a lighter colour. Cut it in half to make the bear's snout and stick to the body.

2. Roll out two little log shapes for the front legs. Cut off one end to make him flat on the ground. Make the back legs with little teardrop shapes. Attach the legs firmly to the body.

3. Use a toothpick to make a vertical line in the bear's snout. Stick a little black ball at the top of the line for his nose.

16

4. Use the point of a pencil to make his mouth. Then stick on two little black balls for his eyes.

5. Now it's time to make his ears. Just flatten two balls and press onto his head. He needs a tail, too, so don't forget to stick a small worm shaped tail on his behind.

Grrrrr . . . I'm really **fierce**

17

1. Start by making a black egg shape. Then make a white ball, flatten it and stick it on for her belly. Smooth it out.

My name is Pippa the **Penguin**

2. Now make two orange teardrop shapes and flatten them for Pippa's feet. Stick them onto the bottom of the egg shape so she can stand up.

3. Make her beak with a small orange teardrop shape. Flatten it and stick it in the middle, overlapping her white belly.

4

5. The wings are two sausage shapes, flattened. Press the top part of each wing onto the body. She looks cuter if the wings stick out a little bit, don't you think?

5

4. To make her eyes, flatten two white balls and stick on. Now press two little black balls into the middle of each one.

make my feet the same size or I'll trip up!

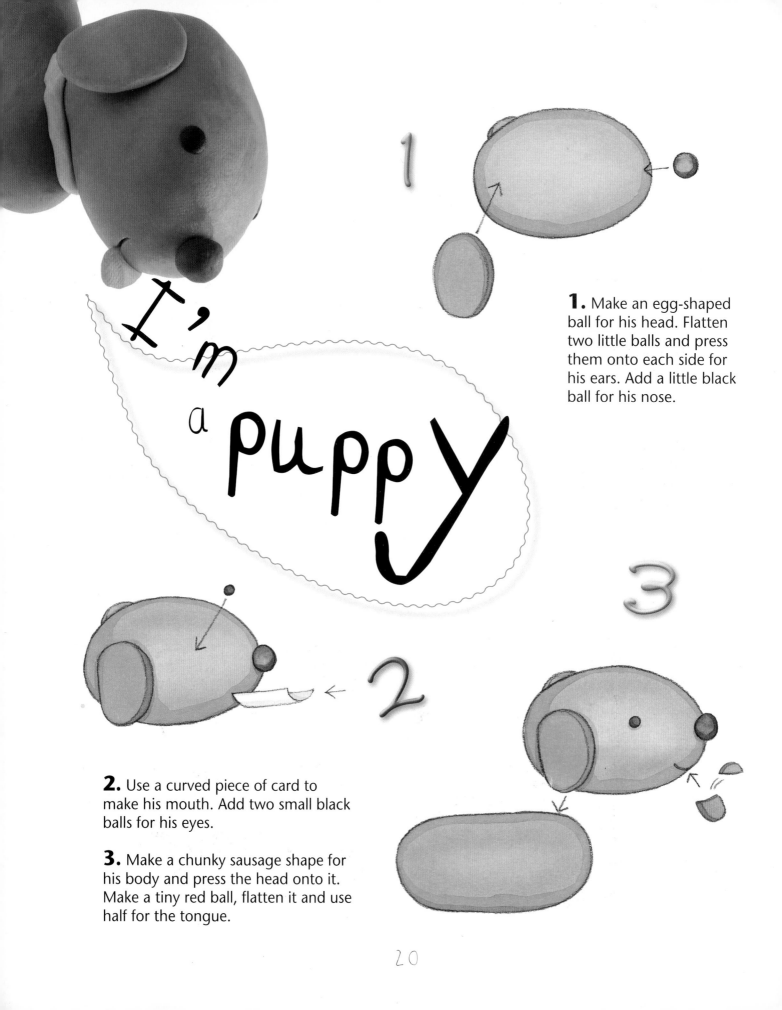

I'm a puppy

1. Make an egg-shaped ball for his head. Flatten two little balls and press them onto each side for his ears. Add a little black ball for his nose.

2. Use a curved piece of card to make his mouth. Add two small black balls for his eyes.

3. Make a chunky sausage shape for his body and press the head onto it. Make a tiny red ball, flatten it and use half for the tongue.

4. Roll out a long skinny worm shape for his collar: it looks really cute and makes the neck joint stronger. And don't forget his tail!

5. For the legs, make a long thin log shape and cut it into four equal pieces. Stick them firmly onto the body.

my tail is up because I'm so happy!

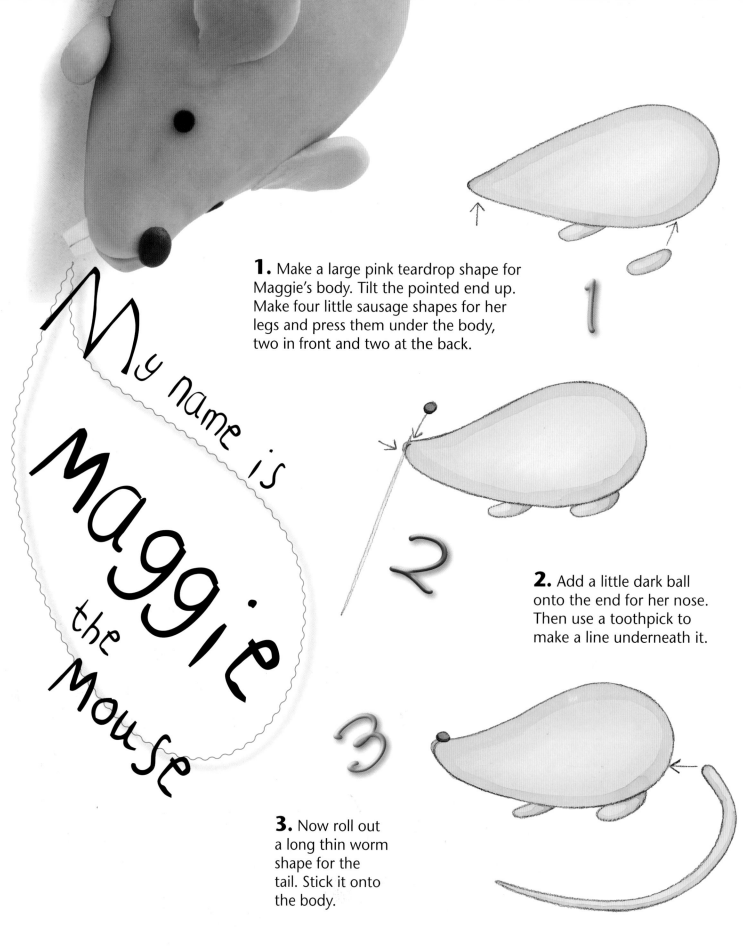

My name is Maggie the Mouse

1. Make a large pink teardrop shape for Maggie's body. Tilt the pointed end up. Make four little sausage shapes for her legs and press them under the body, two in front and two at the back.

2. Add a little dark ball onto the end for her nose. Then use a toothpick to make a line underneath it.

3. Now roll out a long thin worm shape for the tail. Stick it onto the body.

4. Now make her ears by flattening two little pink balls. Press the bottom part onto the head. The tops of the ears should stick out a bit.

5. Add two little black balls for her eyes. Finish off by adding Maggie's front teeth. Cut a small piece of white card, draw a line down the middle and stick in place.

I'd like **white** teeth please

I'm an OWL

1. Roll a large purple ball for the body. Make a flattened lilac-coloured ball for his tummy. Smooth it out well so it blends into the body shape. Then flatten two small white balls and stick them on for the eyes.

2. Make two small purple teardrop shapes for his ears. Stick them on. Then make two little orange teardrop shapes for his feet so your owl can stand up.

3. Another orange teardrop shape works perfectly for his beak. Then press on two small black balls to finish off his eyes.

4. To make the wings, flatten two purple teardrop shapes and stick them onto each side, with the pointed end at the top. Press the top end firmly onto the body.

5. Finish off by creating a feather texture on his tummy using a straw pressed in at an angle.

T-wit T-woo!
I need great big eyes

1. Roll a round ball for his body. Then make a smaller white ball and flatten it. Press it onto the body to make Bengie's belly.

My name is Bengie the Bunny

2. Make four little teardrop shapes for his legs and stick them onto the body (the back legs should be bigger than the front ones). Add a tiny white ball for his tail.

3. Now make two long teardrop shapes for his ears. Flatten them a bit before sticking them on.

26

4. To make his eyes, flatten two white balls and stick them on. Add two little black balls. Attach a little pink ball for his nose and make a short vertical line below it with a toothpick.

5. Make his mouth with the point of a pencil, just below the line. Don't forget to draw on Bengie's whiskers with a toothpick (or use plastic wire).

4

5

Can you make a carrot for me, too?

I'm a bee

1. Roll out a little fat yellow sausage shape for the body. Then roll out a long thin worm shape, between your hands. Flatten it slightly and wrap it around the yellow shape to make your bee's stripey body.

2. Make an orange ball for the head and join it to the body. Make her eyes with two little yellow balls. Add tiny black balls to finish.

3. Add a little red ball for her nose. You can give her blushed cheeks by blending in two flat red disks.

4. Curve a piece of card to make her mouth. Pieces of plastic wire make good antennae.

5. Flatten two little white discs for her wings. Now your buzzy bee just needs legs. Make six mini black teardrop shapes and stick them onto her body.

Bzzzz . . . I love eating nectar!

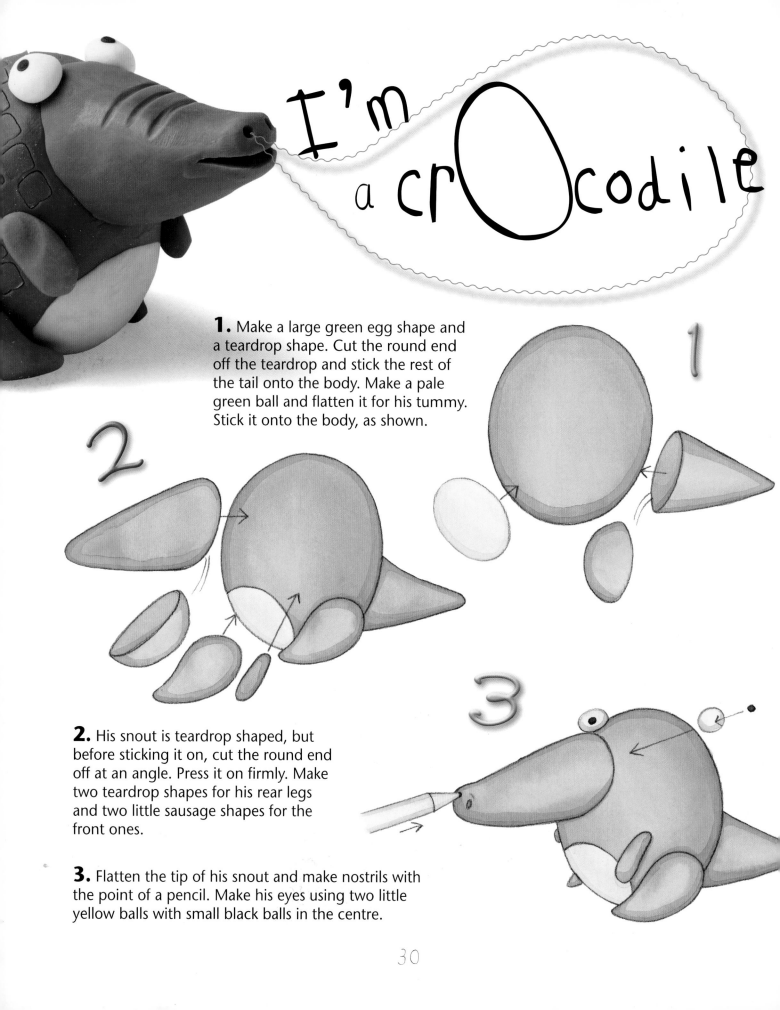

I'm a crOcodile

1. Make a large green egg shape and a teardrop shape. Cut the round end off the teardrop and stick the rest of the tail onto the body. Make a pale green ball and flatten it for his tummy. Stick it onto the body, as shown.

2. His snout is teardrop shaped, but before sticking it on, cut the round end off at an angle. Press it on firmly. Make two teardrop shapes for his rear legs and two little sausage shapes for the front ones.

3. Flatten the tip of his snout and make nostrils with the point of a pencil. Make his eyes using two little yellow balls with small black balls in the centre.

30

4. Use a piece of card to open up his mouth. Add wrinkles to the top of his snout using a toothpick.

4

5. Now you just need to add texture to his skin. Look for a kitchen utensil that you can use to make the same pattern all over his body and tail.

5

I like dancing to rock and roll

1. Start with an egg-shaped body. To make Eddy's legs, roll out a log shape between your hands and cut it into four equal pieces. Stick them onto the body.

My name is Eddy the Elephant

2. Now roll out a log shape for his trunk. Make one end thinner and stick the other end to his body. Push the end of a paintbrush into his trunk to make a hole.

3. For his big ears, make two flat discs and stick them on each side.

5. Elephants have little tails, so add a thin worm shape.

4. Make little black balls for his eyes and don't forget Eddy's tusks! Make two long teardrop shapes in white and stick them on each side of his trunk.

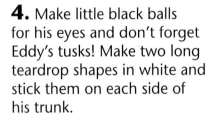

I can waggle my ears!

33

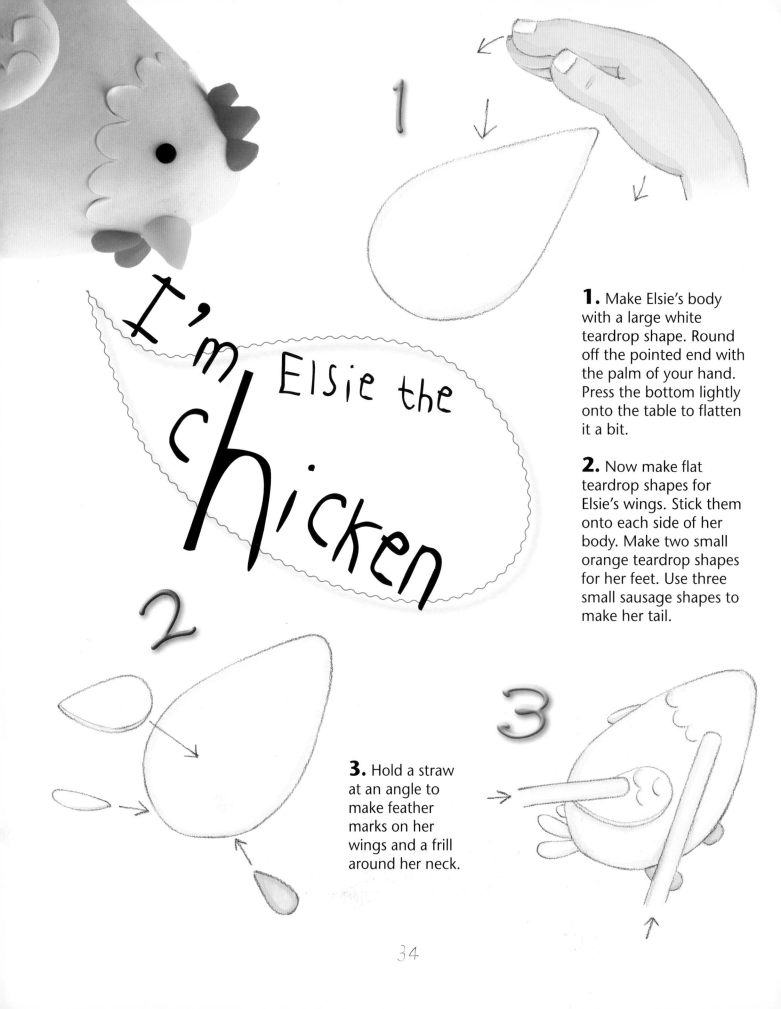

I'm Elsie the chicken

1. Make Elsie's body with a large white teardrop shape. Round off the pointed end with the palm of your hand. Press the bottom lightly onto the table to flatten it a bit.

2. Now make flat teardrop shapes for Elsie's wings. Stick them onto each side of her body. Make two small orange teardrop shapes for her feet. Use three small sausage shapes to make her tail.

3. Hold a straw at an angle to make feather marks on her wings and a frill around her neck.

4. Make her head crest with little red triangles. Add a little teardrop shape for her beak.

5. Stick two little red teardrop shapes below her beak: that's called a wattle. Finally, add two little black balls for eyes. Look, Elsie's ready to lay some eggs!

Cluck, cluck, I can lay an egg for you!

35

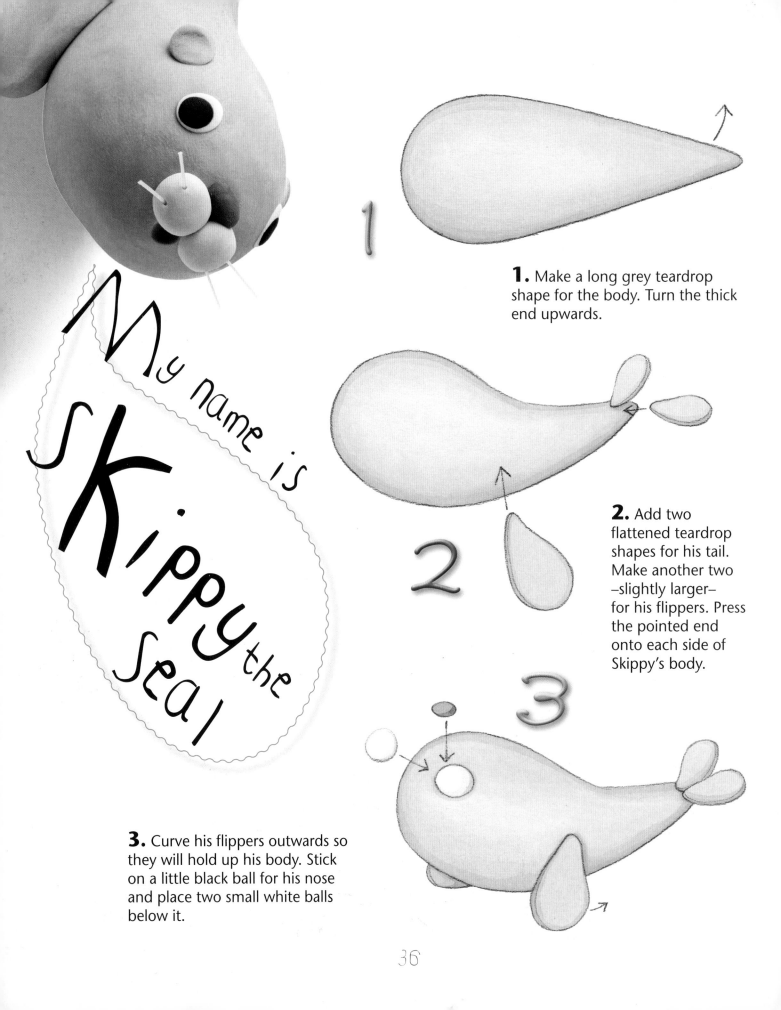

My name is Skippy the Seal

1. Make a long grey teardrop shape for the body. Turn the thick end upwards.

2. Add two flattened teardrop shapes for his tail. Make another two –slightly larger– for his flippers. Press the pointed end onto each side of Skippy's body.

3. Curve his flippers outwards so they will hold up his body. Stick on a little black ball for his nose and place two small white balls below it.

36

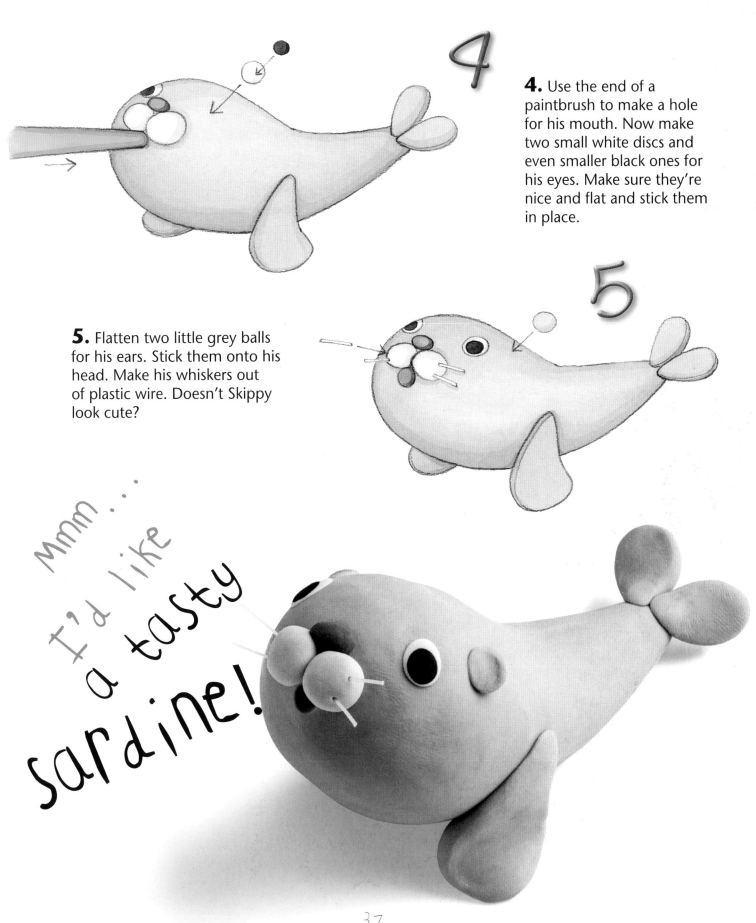

4. Use the end of a paintbrush to make a hole for his mouth. Now make two small white discs and even smaller black ones for his eyes. Make sure they're nice and flat and stick them in place.

5. Flatten two little grey balls for his ears. Stick them onto his head. Make his whiskers out of plastic wire. Doesn't Skippy look cute?

Mmm... I'd like a tasty sardine!

I'm a Frog

1. Make a green egg-shaped body. Add a pale green disc for his tummy.

2. Make his back legs with two flattened green balls. Then roll out a long worm shape and cut it into six pieces for his feet.

1

3. Now make two worm shapes for his front legs. Make them long enough to bend over a bit to hold the frog up. Attach firmly to the body. Make two round green balls for his eyes and stick on.

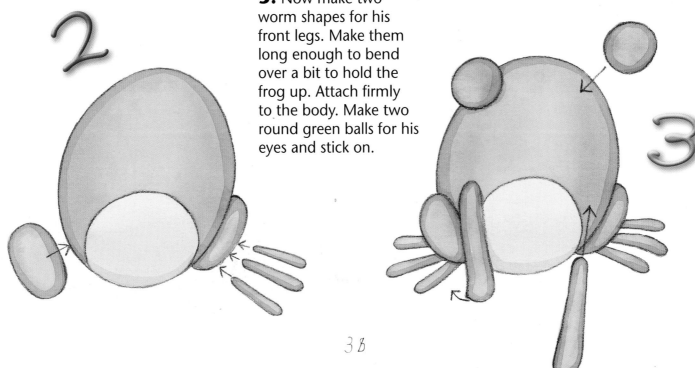

2

3

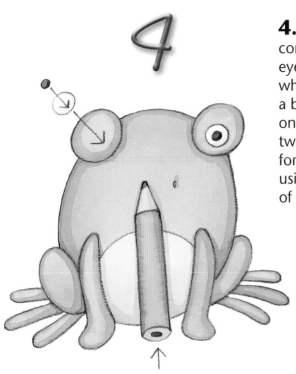

4. To complete each eye, add a white disc with a black ball on top. Make two little holes for his nostrils using the point of a pencil.

5. Now you just need to make his big smiley mouth with a toothpick.

kiss me, please!

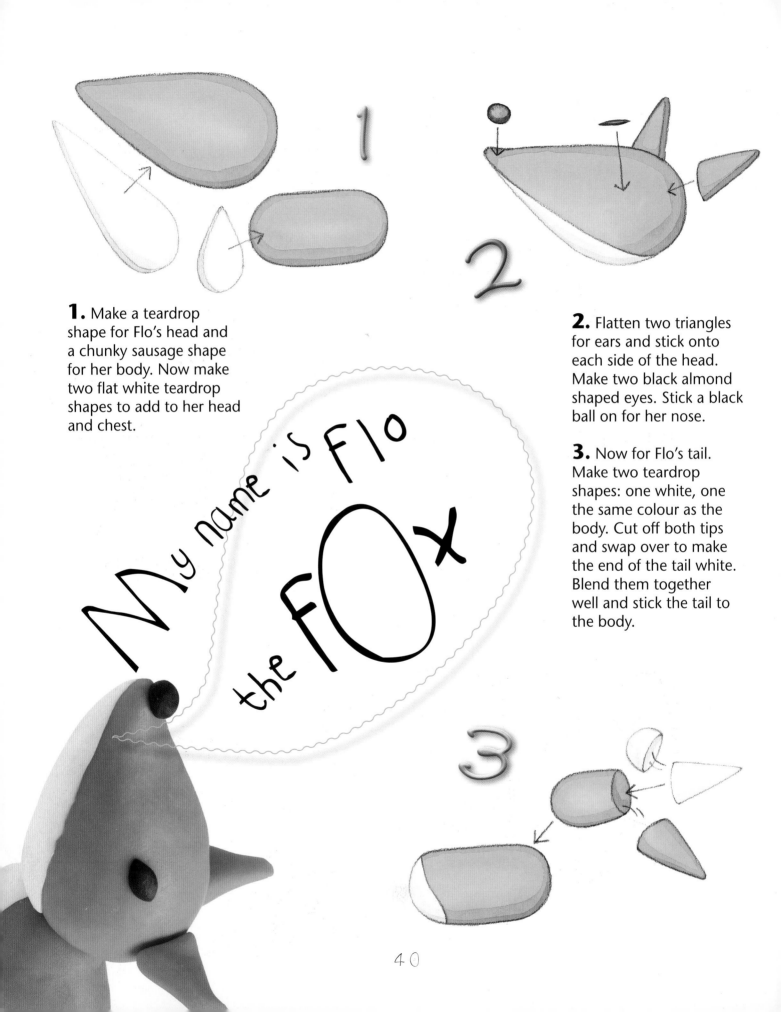

1. Make a teardrop shape for Flo's head and a chunky sausage shape for her body. Now make two flat white teardrop shapes to add to her head and chest.

2. Flatten two triangles for ears and stick onto each side of the head. Make two black almond shaped eyes. Stick a black ball on for her nose.

3. Now for Flo's tail. Make two teardrop shapes: one white, one the same colour as the body. Cut off both tips and swap over to make the end of the tail white. Blend them together well and stick the tail to the body.

My name is Flo the FOX

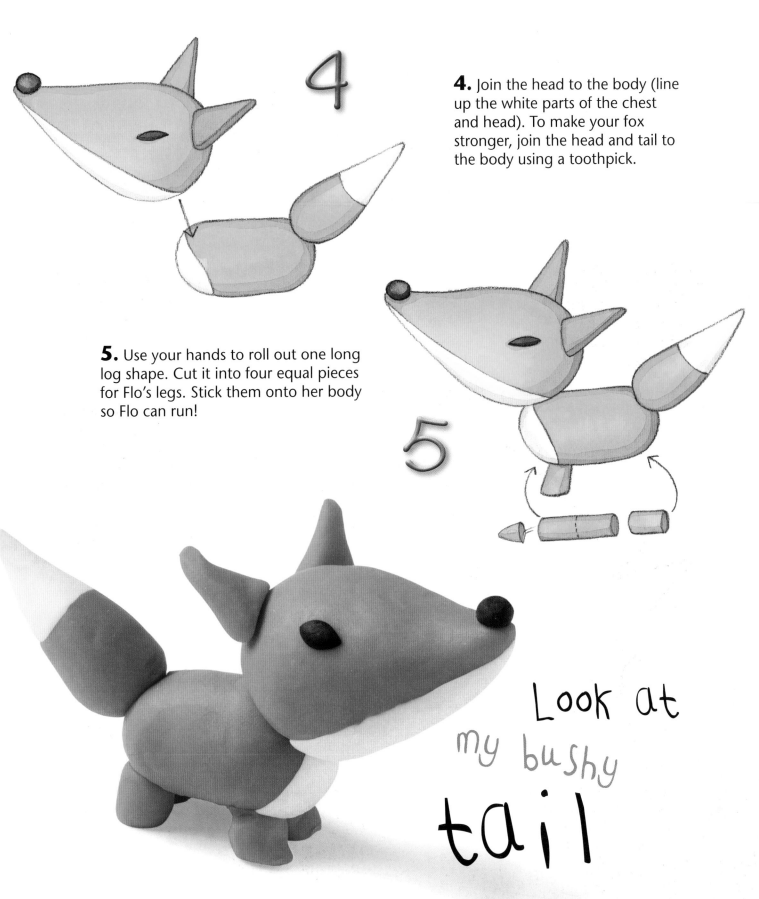

4. Join the head to the body (line up the white parts of the chest and head). To make your fox stronger, join the head and tail to the body using a toothpick.

5. Use your hands to roll out one long log shape. Cut it into four equal pieces for Flo's legs. Stick them onto her body so Flo can run!

Look at my bushy tail

I'm a worm in a yummy apple

1. First make a red ball. Press it lightly onto the table top to flatten the bottom so it stands up. Make a rounded dent in the top with a thick marker pen. Then make a hole in the middle with the point of a pencil and pop in a little brown log shape for the stalk.

2. Now for the worm. Make a little round green ball and a small green log. Join together. Make his mouth using the point of a pencil. Now make his eyes with two small white discs and even smaller black ones.

3. Make another hole with the pencil to stick your hungry worm into.

1. Make a log shape. Roll the tail out thinner and make the front end rounded. Now add bright-coloured discs all over Sammy's body. Curve the body a little bit.

2. Make four teardrop shapes for legs and stick onto both sides of the body. Add his claws using a toothpick.

3. Make a slit for his mouth with a bit of card. Add two nostrils with a toothpick. To finish off, make two round balls for his eyes (the same colour as his spots). Add two flat black discs on top to finish.

My name is Sammy the salamander

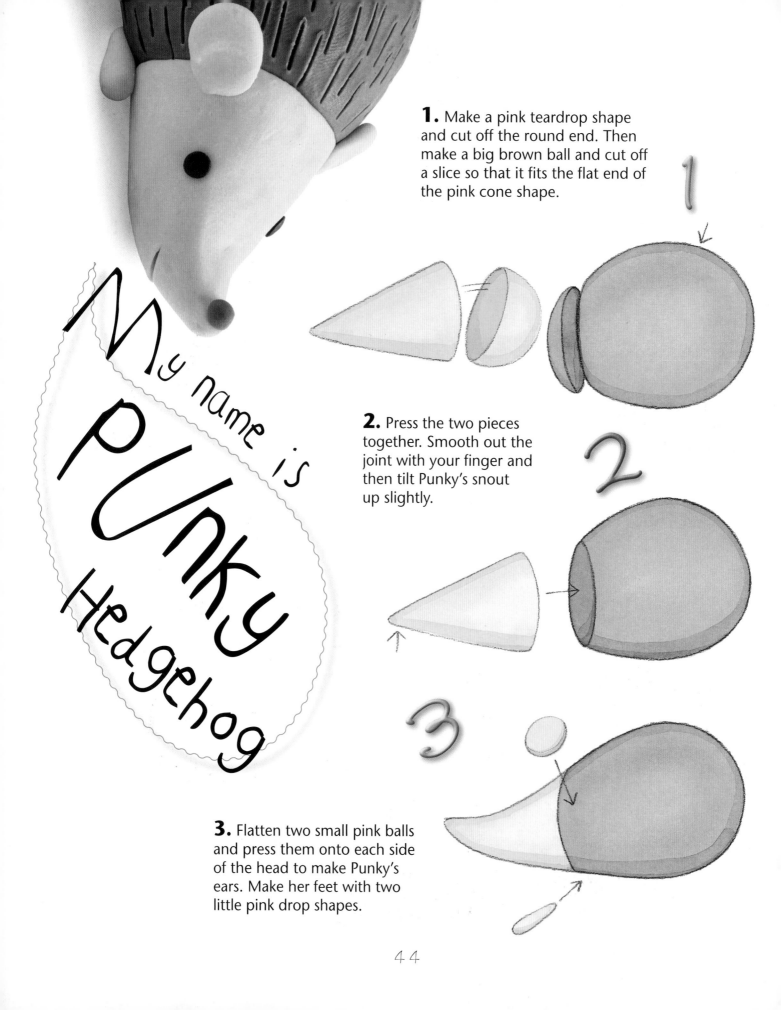

1. Make a pink teardrop shape and cut off the round end. Then make a big brown ball and cut off a slice so that it fits the flat end of the pink cone shape.

2. Press the two pieces together. Smooth out the joint with your finger and then tilt Punky's snout up slightly.

3. Flatten two small pink balls and press them onto each side of the head to make Punky's ears. Make her feet with two little pink drop shapes.

My name is PUNky Hedgehog

44

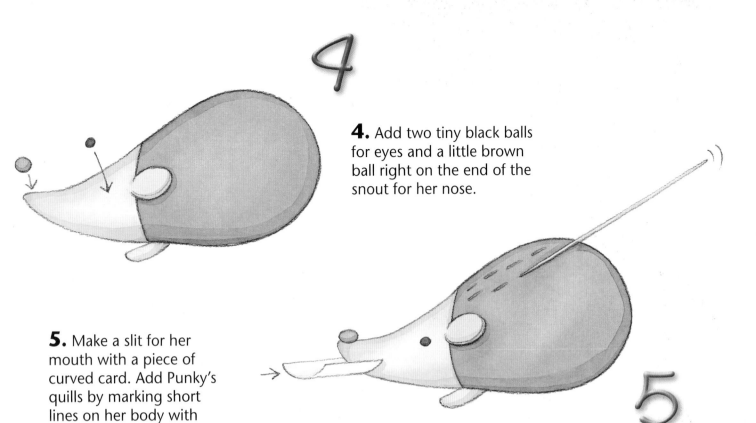

4. Add two tiny black balls for eyes and a little brown ball right on the end of the snout for her nose.

5. Make a slit for her mouth with a piece of curved card. Add Punky's quills by marking short lines on her body with a toothpick.

I've got super cool spikes!

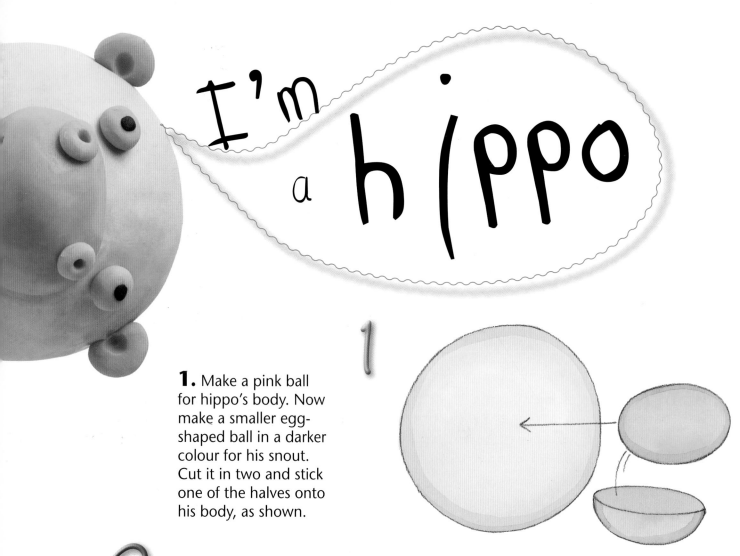

I'm a hippo

1. Make a pink ball for hippo's body. Now make a smaller egg-shaped ball in a darker colour for his snout. Cut it in two and stick one of the halves onto his body, as shown.

2. Roll out a small log shape and cut it in half for his back legs. Stick them onto his body to make him sit up. Make a smaller log and cut it in half for his front legs. Cut all the legs at an angle so the joins fit better.

3. Make his nostrils with two little balls that match his snout. Use a pencil point to make holes in the middle. Use a piece of card to indent the shape of his mouth.

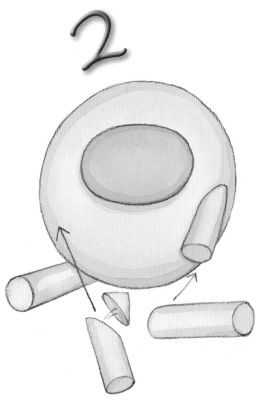

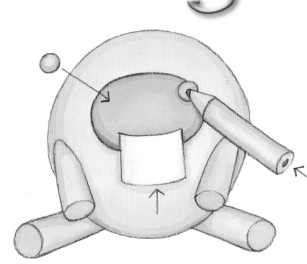

4. Use the same colour again to make two little balls for his ears. Flatten them a little and make a dent in the middle before sticking them onto his head. Another two little balls with black balls added will make his eyes.

5. For his little tail, just stick on a thin sausage shape behind him. As a finishing detail, add little white balls for his toenails.

I love sitting in water!

1. Start by making a ball for Coco's body. Cut off a slice at the top so the head will fit better. Then make a flat white disc for her belly and press it firmly onto the body.

2. Now make two little sausage shapes for the front legs and two larger ones for the back legs.

3. Make a bigger oval-shaped ball for her head. Press it into the body well (a toothpick will strengthen the join). Add a tiny sausage-shaped tail behind.

My name is Coco the **koala**

4

4. Make her nose with a thick log shape. Cut it in half and stick it onto her face. Use two flattened discs for her big ears.

5

5. Finish off by adding two little black balls for her eyes. Now you just need a toothpick to make Coco smile!

I'm very cuddly!

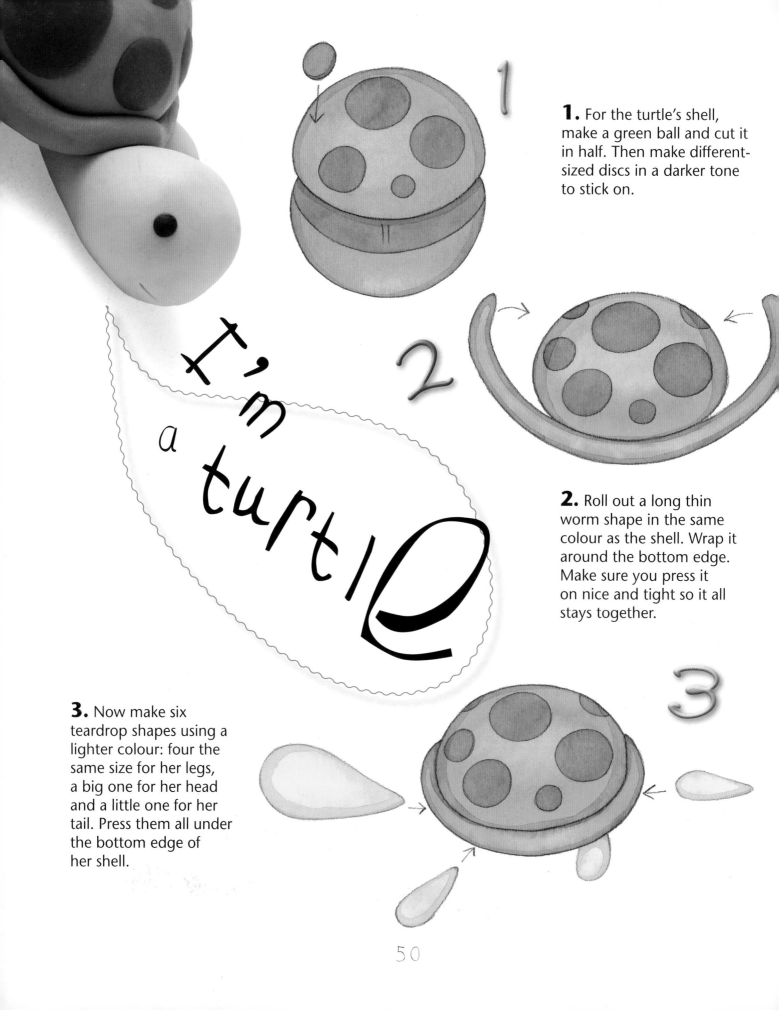

1. For the turtle's shell, make a green ball and cut it in half. Then make different-sized discs in a darker tone to stick on.

2. Roll out a long thin worm shape in the same colour as the shell. Wrap it around the bottom edge. Make sure you press it on nice and tight so it all stays together.

3. Now make six teardrop shapes using a lighter colour: four the same size for her legs, a big one for her head and a little one for her tail. Press them all under the bottom edge of her shell.

I'm a turtle

4. Use a piece of curved thin card to make her mouth.

5. Finish your little turtle by adding two tiny black balls for eyes.

What's the hurry - wait for me!

1. Make two balls using different colours. Cut them both in half and join one half from each colour. Smooth the two halves together well to join them.

My name is Flossie the fish

2. To make Flossie's tail, make a teardrop shape and flatten it. Cut off the pointed end and add some lines with a toothpick. Stick it onto the half with the same colour.

3. Make a small ball for the mouth to match the other half. Stick it on and make a hole in the centre using the end of a paintbrush. Add two small white balls and tiny black ones for her eyes.

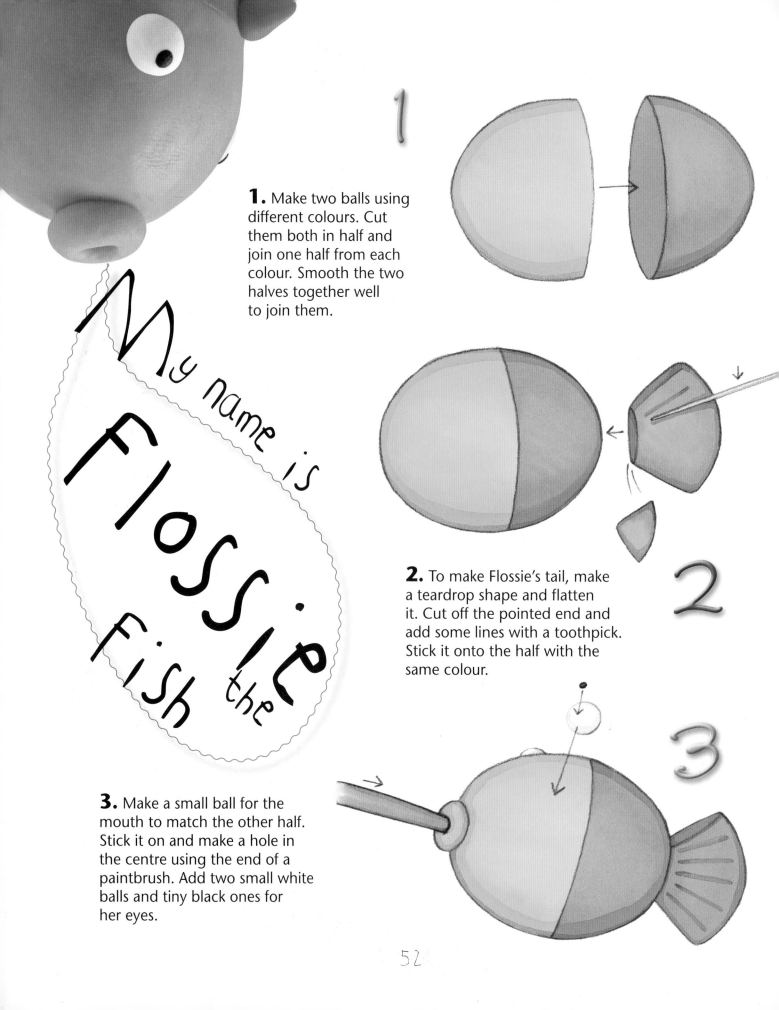

52

4. Holding a straw at an angle, press it into the body to make a fish scale pattern.

5. What would Flossie do without gills? Stick a flattened teardrop shape onto each side of her body. Add lines with a toothpick. Stick three more teardrop shapes on top of her body.

I love swimming!

I'm a Cow

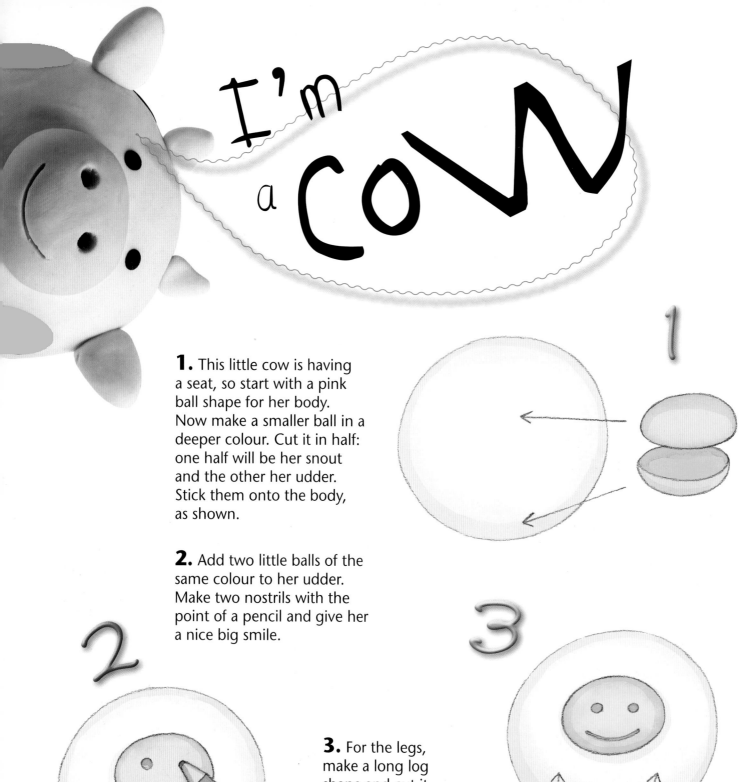

1. This little cow is having a seat, so start with a pink ball shape for her body. Now make a smaller ball in a deeper colour. Cut it in half: one half will be her snout and the other her udder. Stick them onto the body, as shown.

2. Add two little balls of the same colour to her udder. Make two nostrils with the point of a pencil and give her a nice big smile.

3. For the legs, make a long log shape and cut it into four equal pieces. It's best to cut the legs at an angle so they fit well. The back legs are splayed out to support the body.

4. Draw a line onto the back legs to make the hooves. Stick two small teardrop shapes on for her ears. Add two little black balls for her eyes.

5. Now make two little white teardrop shapes for her horns. And don't forget her spotty coat! Use different flattened circle shapes and stick them all over her body.

I say "moo"

1. Making a snake is so easy. Roll out a green worm shape. Then decorate it by pressing on lots of different-sized dark green balls.

2. Coil him up now. Make a small teardrop shape for his head and stick it onto Slinky's body.

3. Make the eyes with two little green balls with black balls on top. Use a toothpick to make his nostrils and use a piece of card to create Slinky's mouth.

My name is Slinky the snake

1. Make a pink ball and eight long teardrop shapes for Ollie's tentacles. Arrange the tentacles around his body. Press them firmly together.

2. Then make three little pink balls. Stick one on for his mouth and make a hole in the middle with the end of a paintbrush. The other two will be his eyes.

3. Stick two little black balls on to finish off the eyes. Now make lots of different-sized balls in another colour. Stick them on all over Ollie's body.

I'm Ollie the octopus

I'm a Kitten

1. If you want to create a Siamese kitten, mix white modelling clay with a bit of yellow, brown and a little blue. Make this colour into two balls and join them together. The head should be bigger than the body. (Use a toothpick to strengthen the join.)

2. Stick a tiny black ball in the middle of the head for her little nose. Stick two little dark brown balls, flattened, underneath.

3. Draw a short vertical line under the nose and then add the mouth, using a toothpick. Hold a straw at an angle to create her closed eyes. Shhh, she's sleeping…

4

5

4. For her ears, make two flattened teardrop shapes in dark brown. You can use plastic wire to make her whiskers.

5. The front paws are made with two sausage shapes, the same colour as the body. Stick them under her head. Make a dark brown sausage shape for her tail. Curl this around her body.

Zzzz...

I'm

purr...fectly

comfy

here...

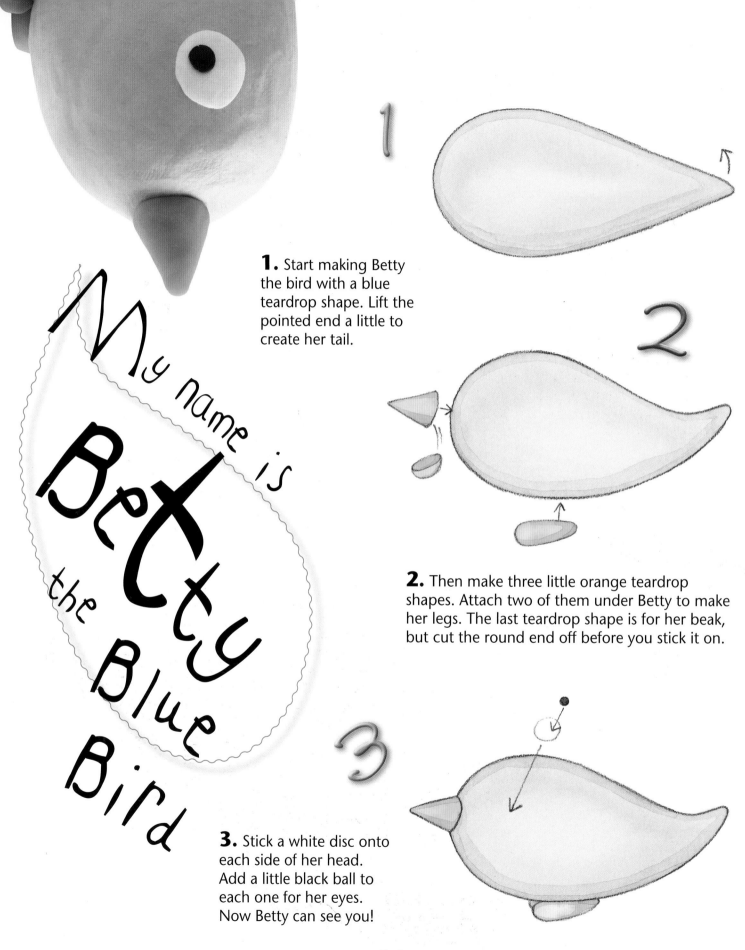

My name is **Betty** the **Blue Bird**

1. Start making Betty the bird with a blue teardrop shape. Lift the pointed end a little to create her tail.

2. Then make three little orange teardrop shapes. Attach two of them under Betty to make her legs. The last teardrop shape is for her beak, but cut the round end off before you stick it on.

3. Stick a white disc onto each side of her head. Add a little black ball to each one for her eyes. Now Betty can see you!

4. Make two flat teardrop shapes for the wings, one on each side. Use a darker tone than the body or even a different colour. You choose!

5. Finish off Betty's wings by adding a feather pattern. Hold a straw at a slant and press lightly into the modelling clay. Now perhaps she'll sing you a song!

Tweet, tweet . . .

I'm a little Chick

1. Make an egg-shaped yellow ball for his body and two little orange teardrop shapes for his feet. Place the feet under the body and press down lightly so that he stands up well.

2. To make the beak, make a little orange teardrop shape. Press it on with your finger.

3. Stick on two little white discs for the eyes.

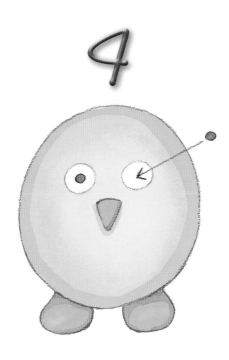

4 *4.* Don't forget to finish off the eyes by adding little black balls in the middle.

5. Make two slightly-flattened oval shapes for your little chick's wings. Press the tops of the wings to the body, leaving the other ends free.

5

Can you make a mum for me?

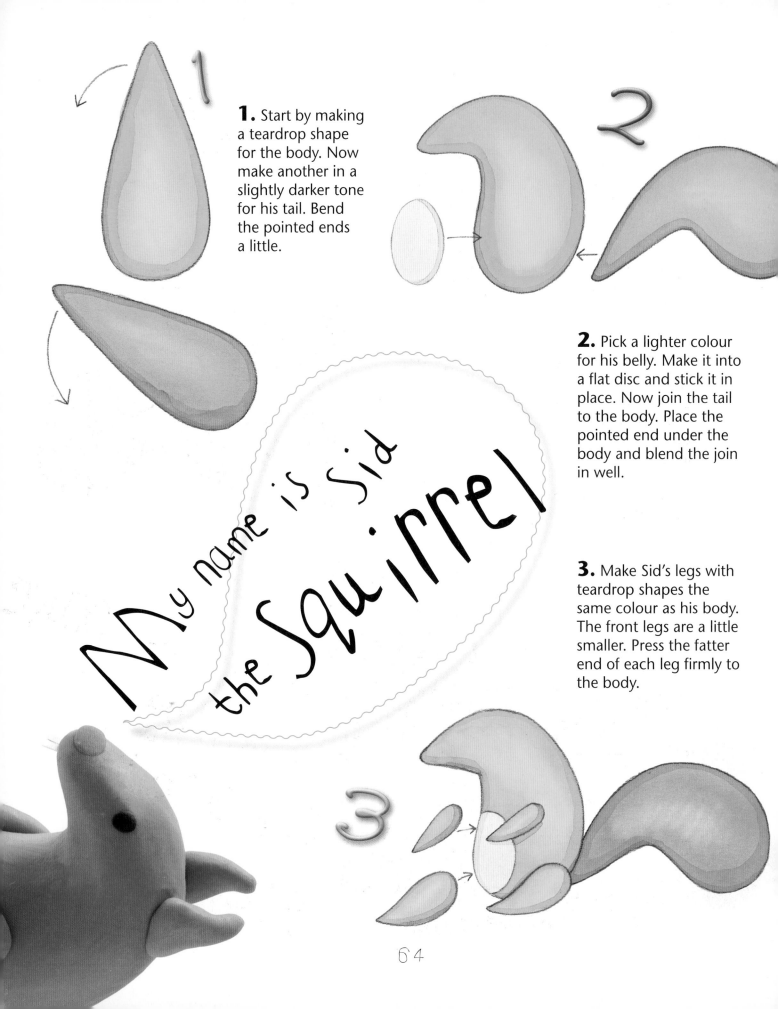

1. Start by making a teardrop shape for the body. Now make another in a slightly darker tone for his tail. Bend the pointed ends a little.

2. Pick a lighter colour for his belly. Make it into a flat disc and stick it in place. Now join the tail to the body. Place the pointed end under the body and blend the join in well.

3. Make Sid's legs with teardrop shapes the same colour as his body. The front legs are a little smaller. Press the fatter end of each leg firmly to the body.

My name is Sid the Squirrel

4. Now make two little teardrop shapes for Sid's ears. Add a tiny little ball the same colour as the tail for his nose.

5. To finish off, add two little black balls for Sid's eyes. And most important – he needs strong teeth! Cut out some thin card for teeth and press them into the clay as shown. Without them Sid couldn't eat his dinner!

Can you make me an acorn, please?

I'm a ladybird

1

1. Start by making a red ball and then flatten it slightly with the palm of your hand. Now make a flat pink disc and press it over one end of the body to make her face.

2. Draw a line along her back. Press lots of little black balls all over to give her a spotty body.

2

3

3. For eyes, stick two little black balls onto two white discs. Press a curved piece of card into the clay to give her a lovely smile.

4. Add a little red ball for her nose. For her antennae, you could use two pieces of black nylon thread or wire.

5. Now she needs six legs. Make a long, thin black worm shape and cut it into six pieces. Add three to each side of her body. That was easy, wasn't it?

Do you like my spotty dress?

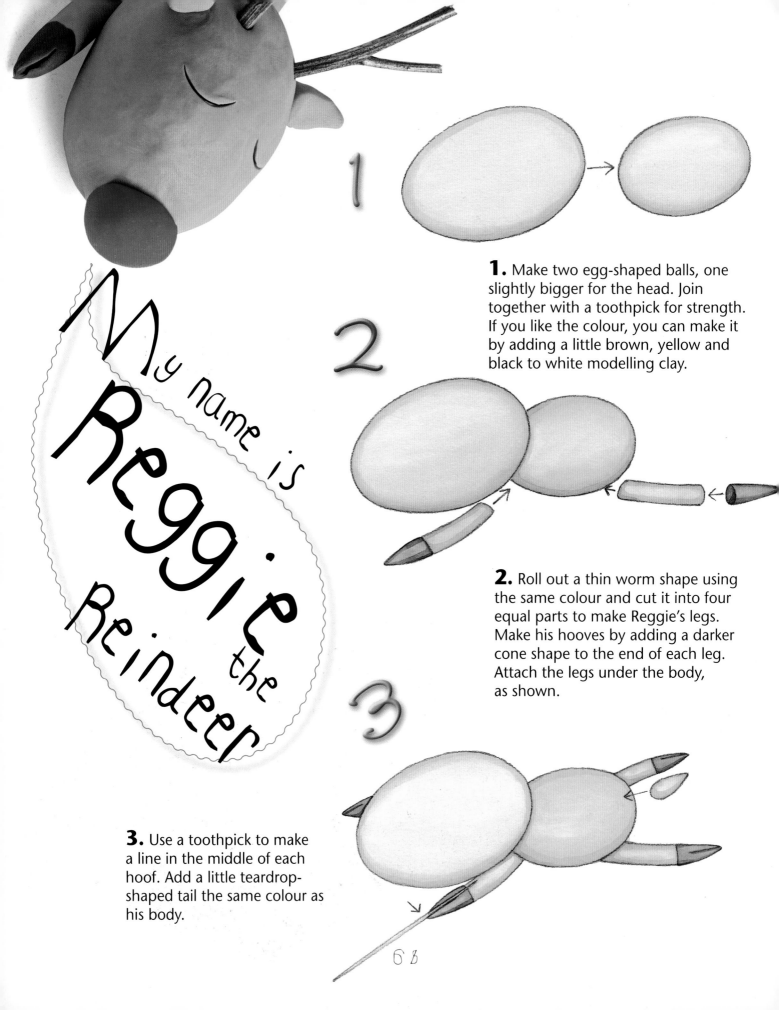

My name is
Reggie the
Reindeer

1. Make two egg-shaped balls, one slightly bigger for the head. Join together with a toothpick for strength. If you like the colour, you can make it by adding a little brown, yellow and black to white modelling clay.

2. Roll out a thin worm shape using the same colour and cut it into four equal parts to make Reggie's legs. Make his hooves by adding a darker cone shape to the end of each leg. Attach the legs under the body, as shown.

3. Use a toothpick to make a line in the middle of each hoof. Add a little teardrop-shaped tail the same colour as his body.

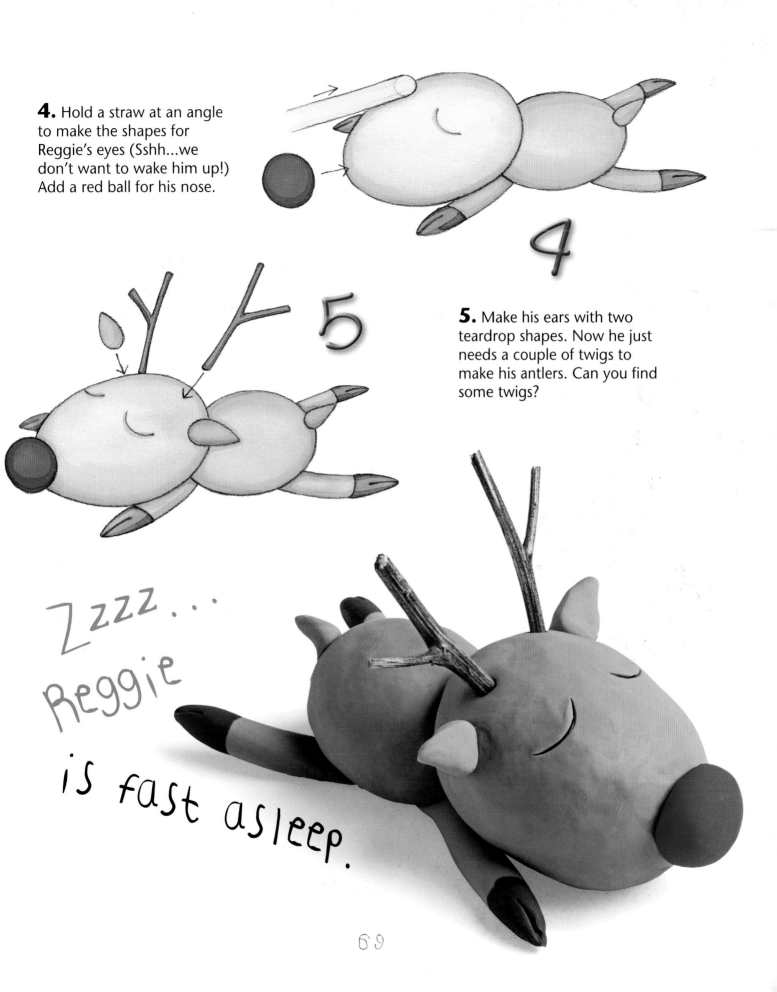

4. Hold a straw at an angle to make the shapes for Reggie's eyes (Sshh...we don't want to wake him up!) Add a red ball for his nose.

4

5

5. Make his ears with two teardrop shapes. Now he just needs a couple of twigs to make his antlers. Can you find some twigs?

Zzzz...

Reggie

is fast asleep.

I'm a toucan

1. Make a black ball for the toucan's body. Then press a white disc onto it to make his belly.

2. Make a flat black teardrop shape for his tail and two flat balls for his legs. These will help Mr Toucan to stand up.

3. Toucans have huge orange beaks. Make a teardrop shape and cut off the round end before you stick it on. Finish off the tail by making a line down the middle with a toothpick.

70

4. Curve the end of the beak down a little, as shown. To make his eyes, stick on two blue discs and add a little black ball in the middle.

5. Finish off by adding a wing to each side of Mr Toucan's body. Make a flattened teardrop shape for each wing.

What
a
beak!

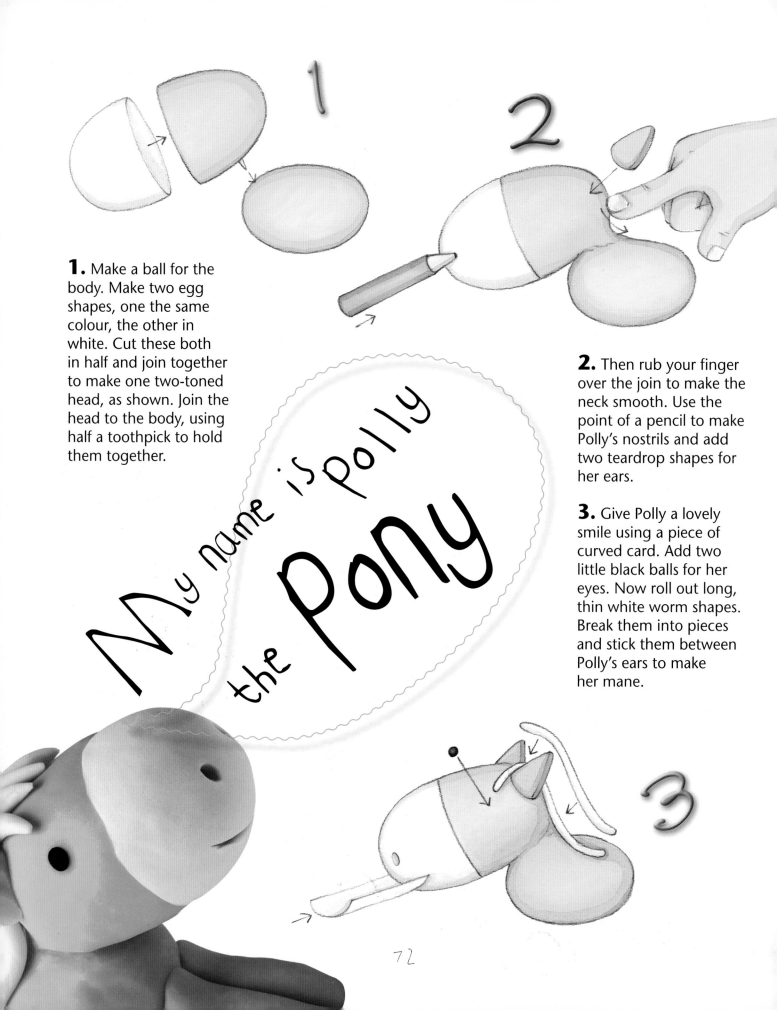

1 *1* *2*

1. Make a ball for the body. Make two egg shapes, one the same colour, the other in white. Cut these both in half and join together to make one two-toned head, as shown. Join the head to the body, using half a toothpick to hold them together.

2. Then rub your finger over the join to make the neck smooth. Use the point of a pencil to make Polly's nostrils and add two teardrop shapes for her ears.

3. Give Polly a lovely smile using a piece of curved card. Add two little black balls for her eyes. Now roll out long, thin white worm shapes. Break them into pieces and stick them between Polly's ears to make her mane.

My name is Polly the Pony

3

72

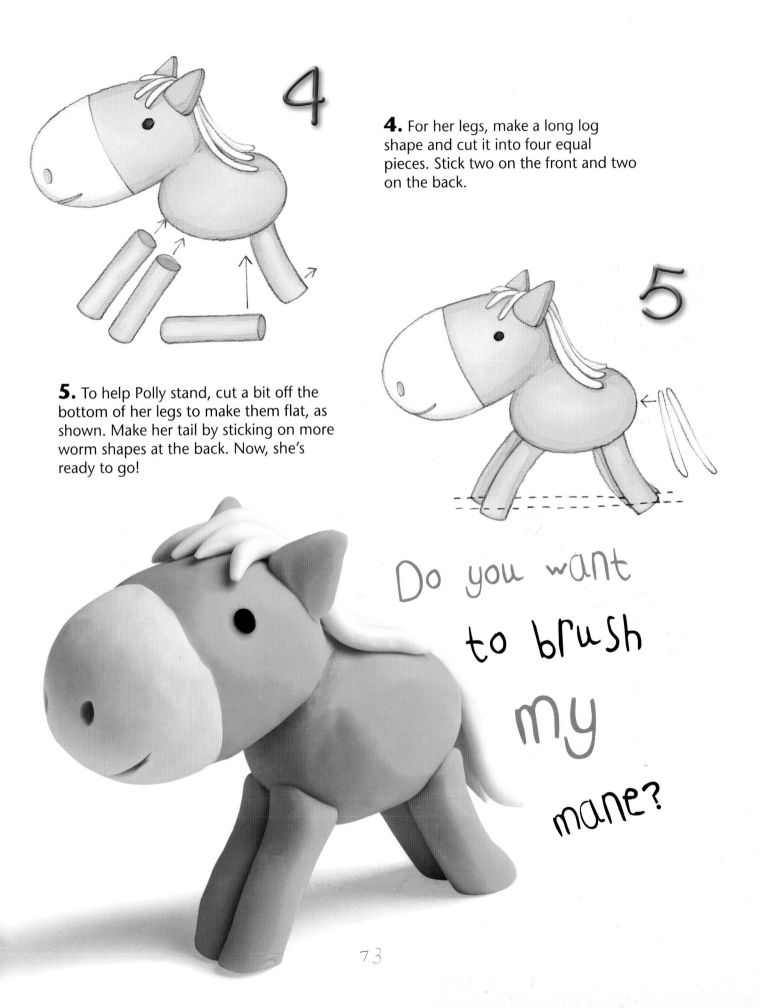

4. For her legs, make a long log shape and cut it into four equal pieces. Stick two on the front and two on the back.

5. To help Polly stand, cut a bit off the bottom of her legs to make them flat, as shown. Make her tail by sticking on more worm shapes at the back. Now, she's ready to go!

Do you want to brush my mane?

1. Make two white balls, one smaller than the other for the body. Join them together firmly (use a toothpick if you want).

2. Roll out a black log shape. Wrap it around panda's neck like a scarf, so that the ends create her front legs. Blend it in at the back with your finger so everything is joined together well. For the back legs, make two black teardrop shapes and wedge under the body to hold him up.

3. Make a small white ball and cut it in half for his snout. Make two black balls, flatten them and stick them to the top of his head.

I'm a panda

4. Add a little black ball for panda's nose. Finish off by making a vertical line with a toothpick.

4

5

5. And now, careful with his eyes. Start by making two black flat oval discs and stick them onto his face. Then add two little white balls in the middle and finish with two more tiny black balls.

I can eat bamboo all day long

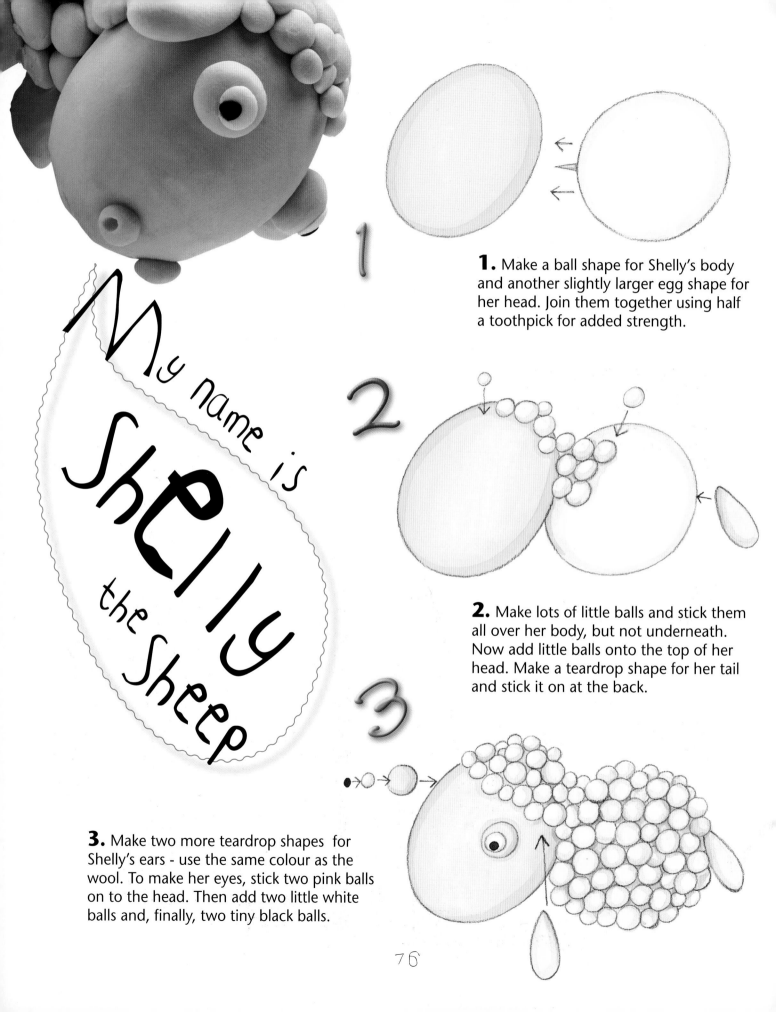

My name is Shelly the Sheep

1

1. Make a ball shape for Shelly's body and another slightly larger egg shape for her head. Join them together using half a toothpick for added strength.

2

2. Make lots of little balls and stick them all over her body, but not underneath. Now add little balls onto the top of her head. Make a teardrop shape for her tail and stick it on at the back.

3

3. Make two more teardrop shapes for Shelly's ears - use the same colour as the wool. To make her eyes, stick two pink balls on to the head. Then add two little white balls and, finally, two tiny black balls.

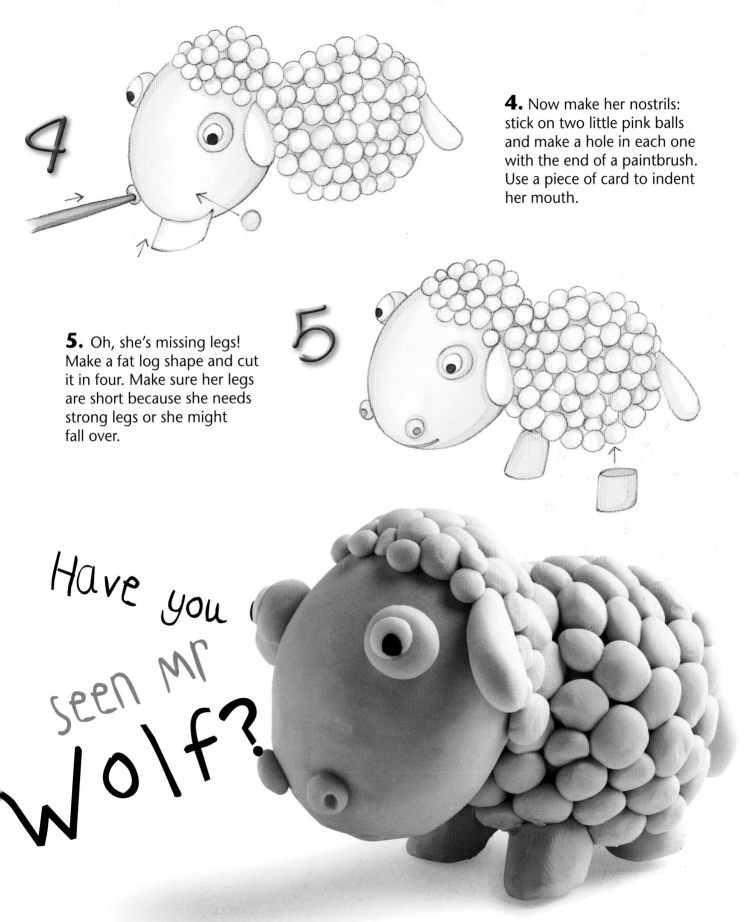

4. Now make her nostrils: stick on two little pink balls and make a hole in each one with the end of a paintbrush. Use a piece of card to indent her mouth.

5. Oh, she's missing legs! Make a fat log shape and cut it in four. Make sure her legs are short because she needs strong legs or she might fall over.

Have you seen Mr Wolf?

I'm a hamster

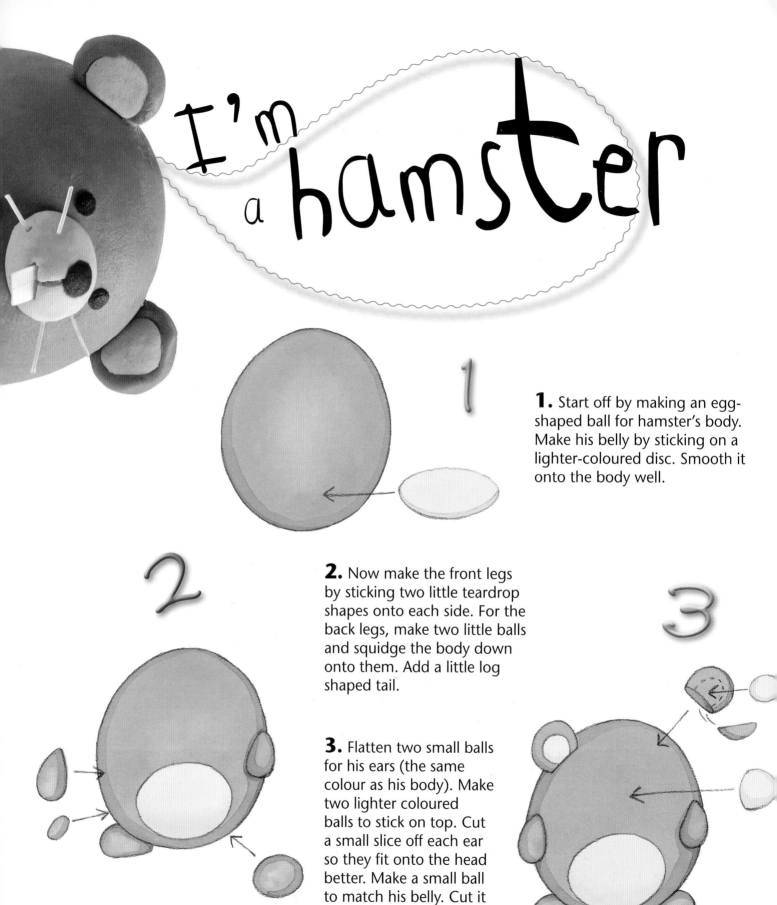

1. Start off by making an egg-shaped ball for hamster's body. Make his belly by sticking on a lighter-coloured disc. Smooth it onto the body well.

2. Now make the front legs by sticking two little teardrop shapes onto each side. For the back legs, make two little balls and squidge the body down onto them. Add a little log shaped tail.

3. Flatten two small balls for his ears (the same colour as his body). Make two lighter coloured balls to stick on top. Cut a small slice off each ear so they fit onto the head better. Make a small ball to match his belly. Cut it in half to make his snout.

78

4. Stick a little black ball in the middle for his nose and make a vertical line below it using a toothpick. Make two more little black balls for his eyes.

5. And now to finish him off, cut a small piece of card to make his teeth. Add little pieces of plastic wire to make his whiskers.

I'm hungry... Is it time for lunch?

1. Start by making four blue balls for Betsy's wings. Make two bigger than the others. Flatten them and decorate them with lots of little balls in a different colour. If you have a roller, it will make her wings nice and flat.

2. Put the little wings behind the big ones, as shown. Then make a long, skinny teardrop shape and stick it onto the wings for her body. Blend them in well at the back to join them.

My name is Betsy the Butterfly

3. Holding a straw at an angle, press it into the body for her mouth.

4

4. Make two little blue balls for Betsy's eyes and then add two more tiny black balls. You can make her nose with a little piece of plastic wire.

5. For her antennae, use pieces of plastic wire. Finish off by sticking on six skinny little shapes for her legs. Meet Betsy!

5

Do you like my pretty spots?

81

My name is **Mickey the monkey**

1. Make a big ball for Mickey's head, then add a flat disc in a lighter colour for his face. Stick two flat discs on each side of his head for ears.

2. Stick on two little black balls for his eyes. Use a toothpick to add a short line, as shown.

3. Now add a little ball for his nose and make a hole for his mouth using the point of a pencil.

4. Make a chunky barrel shape for his body. Join it to the head and flatten it slightly onto the table top so he can sit up.

5. Now roll out a long thin worm shape. Cut it into pieces: two for the front arms, two longer pieces for the back legs and the longest piece for his tail. Make his legs long enough to bend at the knee, as shown. Stick all these pieces on.

I'm having a rest

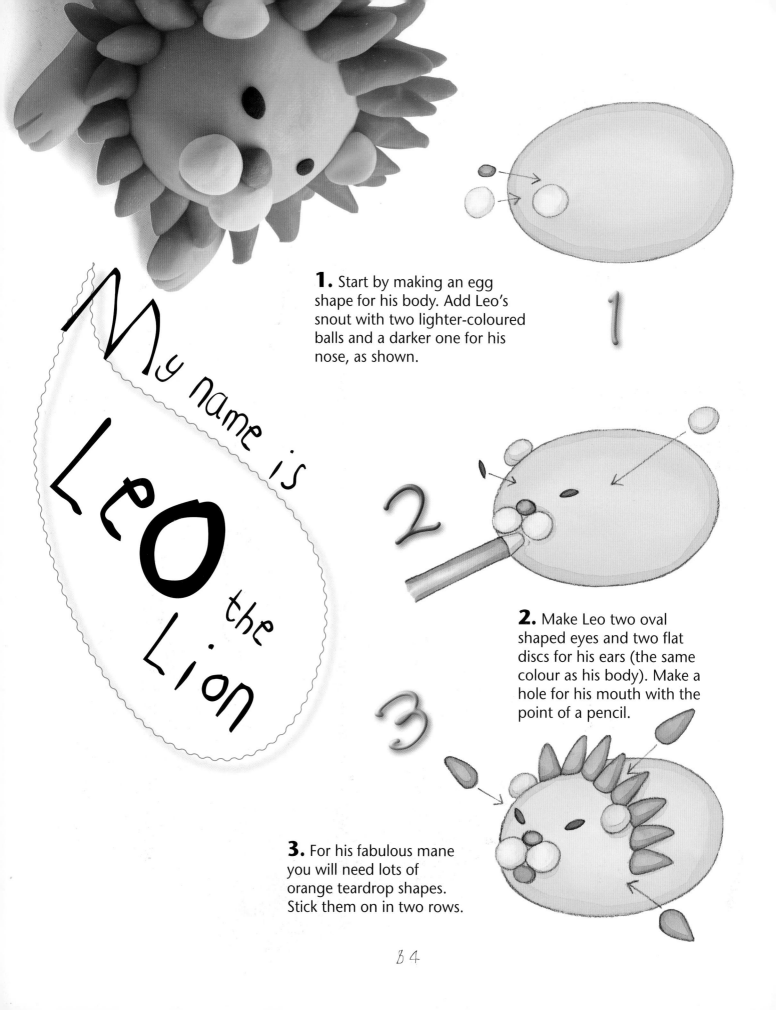

My name is LeO the Lion

1. Start by making an egg shape for his body. Add Leo's snout with two lighter-coloured balls and a darker one for his nose, as shown.

1

2

2. Make Leo two oval shaped eyes and two flat discs for his ears (the same colour as his body). Make a hole for his mouth with the point of a pencil.

3

3. For his fabulous mane you will need lots of orange teardrop shapes. Stick them on in two rows.

4. Make two sausage shapes for his front legs and two teardrop shapes for his back legs.

5. Stick all four legs to the body. Then add sharp claws to Leo's front paws using a toothpick. To make his tail, roll out a worm shape the same colour as the body and add an orange teardrop shape to the tip.

I've got a very loud... roar!

I'm Rocky raccOon

1. Roll out a chunky barrel shape for his body. Cut off the ends to make them flat. Make a flat white oval for his tummy and stick it onto the body. Make his head a big egg shape. Make his eye mask by overlapping two flat black discs on his face, as shown.

2. Join the head and body together. Now stick on two small white discs and even smaller black ones to make his eyes.

3. Make two little sausage shapes for his front legs in the same colour as his body. His back legs are made with two black teardrop shapes.

4. Use a piece of card to make Rocky's mouth. Make his ears by sticking two little black triangles onto slightly bigger ones that match the colour of his head. Stick them on. Don't forget to add his nose!

5. Now he just needs his stripey tail. Roll out a white teardrop shape and wrap flattened black strips around it. Blend them together by rolling it on the table top and then stick it onto his body.

I've got my eyes on you . . .

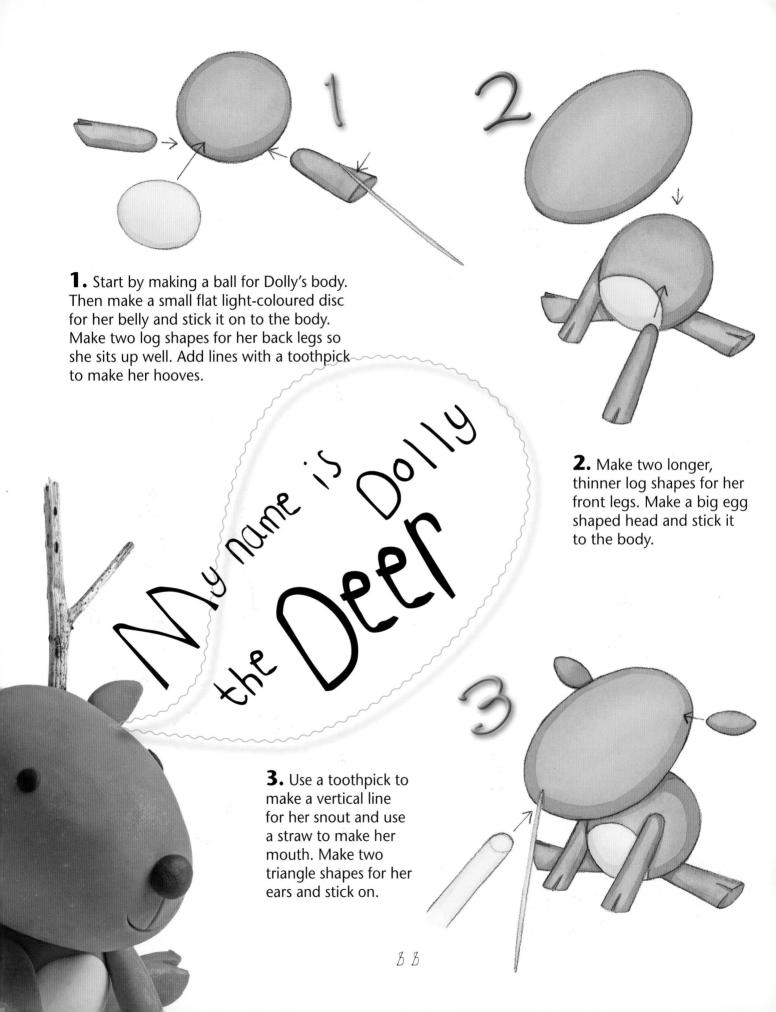

1. Start by making a ball for Dolly's body. Then make a small flat light-coloured disc for her belly and stick it on to the body. Make two log shapes for her back legs so she sits up well. Add lines with a toothpick to make her hooves.

2. Make two longer, thinner log shapes for her front legs. Make a big egg shaped head and stick it to the body.

3. Use a toothpick to make a vertical line for her snout and use a straw to make her mouth. Make two triangle shapes for her ears and stick on.

My name is Dolly the Deer

88

4. Give Dolly a black nose and make her eyes with little black balls. Flatten the eyeballs a little bit.

5. Stick on a little teardrop shape behind her for her tail. Make Dolly's spotty coat by adding a few balls in the same colour as her belly. Press them flat onto her body. Find two little twigs to make Dolly's antlers.

My antlers are beautiful!

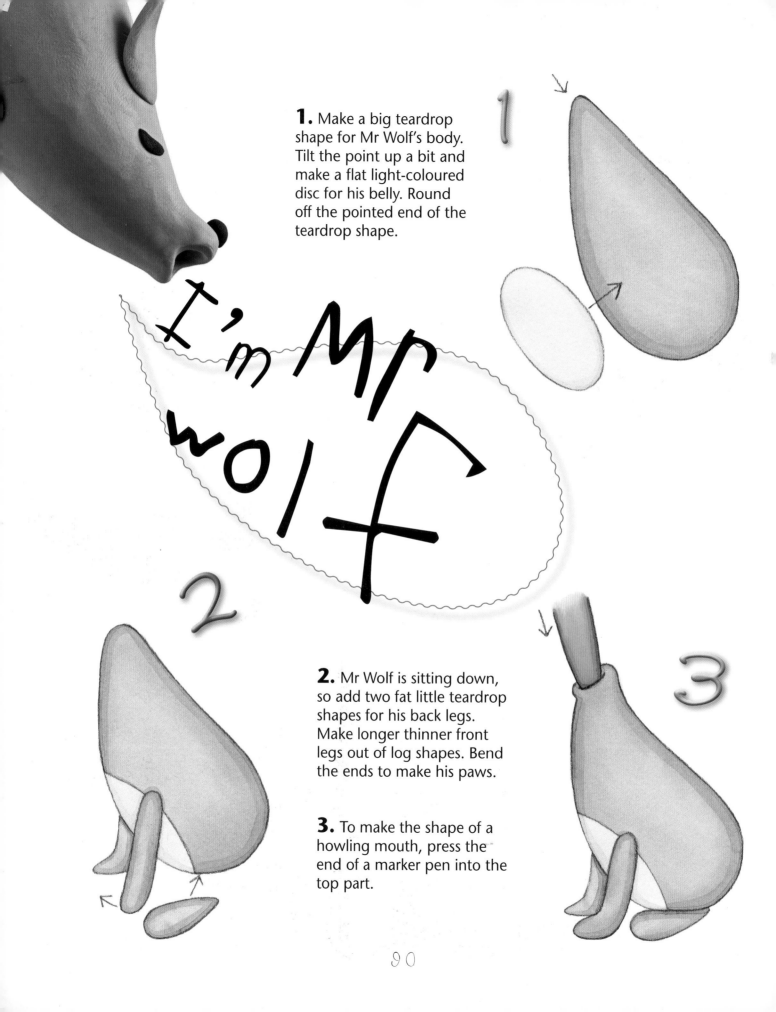

1. Make a big teardrop shape for Mr Wolf's body. Tilt the point up a bit and make a flat light-coloured disc for his belly. Round off the pointed end of the teardrop shape.

2. Mr Wolf is sitting down, so add two fat little teardrop shapes for his back legs. Make longer thinner front legs out of log shapes. Bend the ends to make his paws.

3. To make the shape of a howling mouth, press the end of a marker pen into the top part.

I'm Mr wolf

4. Add two flattened teardrop shapes for his ears. Make his tail with a fat worm shape that is pointed at both ends. Place the tail under his body and smooth the clay together to join.

5. Add a little black ball for his nose and two little black half-moon shapes for his eyes. Now Mr Wolf is complete.

Ar-rooo!

91

I'm Mama kangaroo

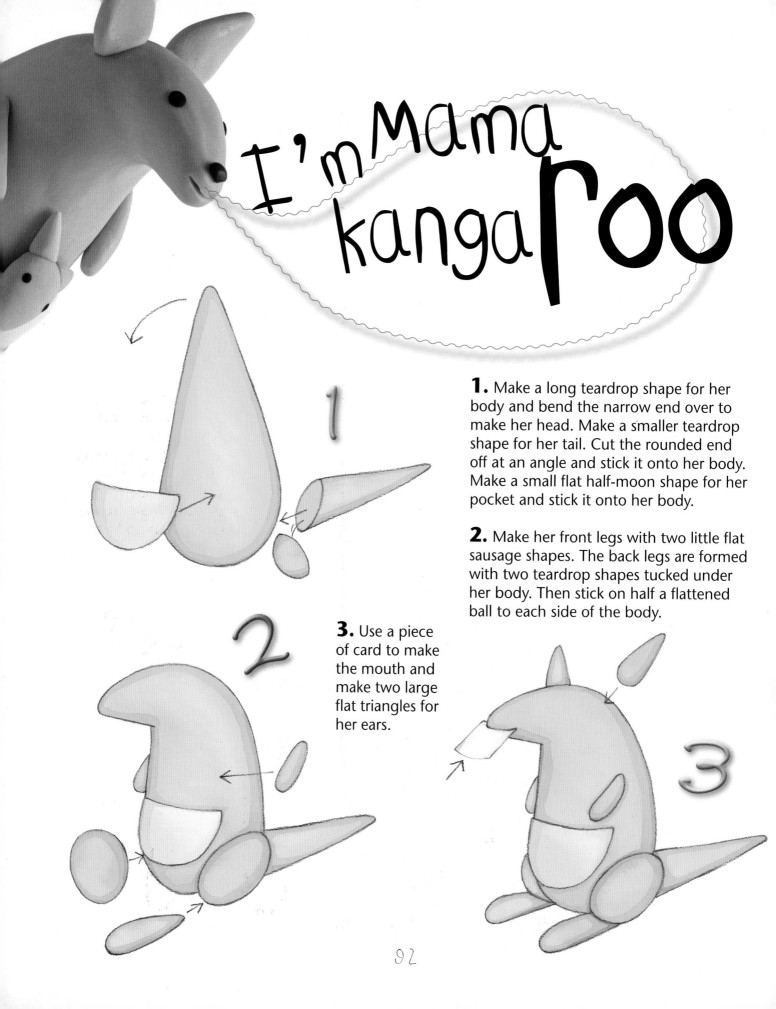

1. Make a long teardrop shape for her body and bend the narrow end over to make her head. Make a smaller teardrop shape for her tail. Cut the rounded end off at an angle and stick it onto her body. Make a small flat half-moon shape for her pocket and stick it onto her body.

2. Make her front legs with two little flat sausage shapes. The back legs are formed with two teardrop shapes tucked under her body. Then stick on half a flattened ball to each side of the body.

3. Use a piece of card to make the mouth and make two large flat triangles for her ears.

4. Now you need three little black balls: two flattened ones for her eyes and a round one for her nose.

5. Mama kangaroo is all done now, but where's her little baby? Make little drop shapes for his head and ears and stick on tiny black balls for the baby's nose and eyes.

My little joey is nice and cosy

93

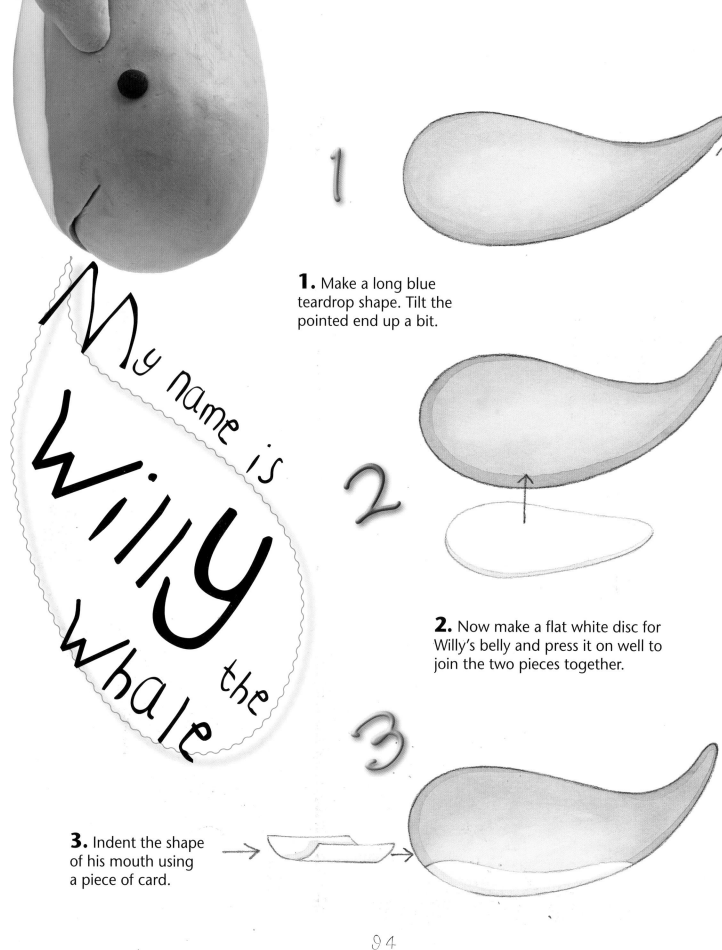

My name is Willy the Whale

1. Make a long blue teardrop shape. Tilt the pointed end up a bit.

2. Now make a flat white disc for Willy's belly and press it on well to join the two pieces together.

3. Indent the shape of his mouth using a piece of card.

4. Press two little black balls on for Willy's eyes.

5. Make his fins with two flattened teardrop shapes. Stick the pointed end onto each side. Now do the same for the tail. Blend the shapes into the body to strengthen the join.

I'm off for a swim . . .

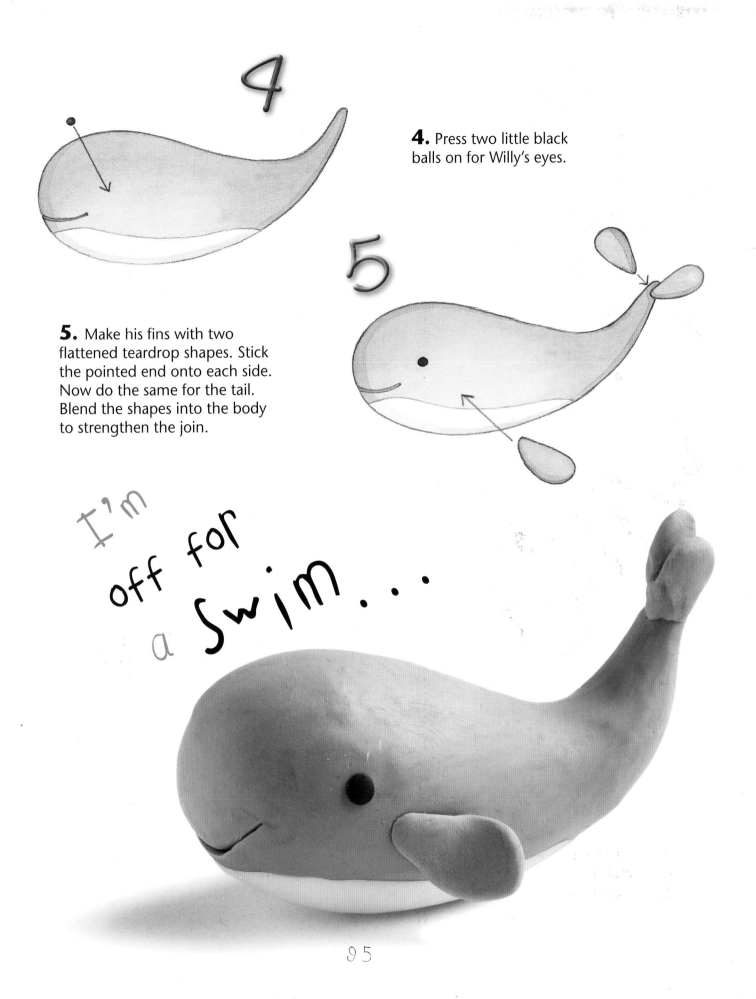

95

Glossary

Almond The seed of the almond tree. It's oval-shaped with pointed ends.

Modelling clay Used to sculpt three-dimensional shapes and figures.

Wire A flexible, thin thread.

Dinosaur Enormous extinct species of reptile that lived more than 65 million years ago.

Raccoon A grey-furred mammal native to North America.

Disc A flat circular object.

Salamander An amphibian with a brightly-coloured body.

Toothpick A short pointed wooden or plastic stick used to remove bits of food stuck between the teeth.

Indent A groove in an object.

Tentacle A flexible limb used by an animal to move around, hold things and sense its surroundings.

Toucan A brightly-coloured bird with a large beak. It lives in the tropics and eats fruit.